T0086705

Central America and the Caribbean

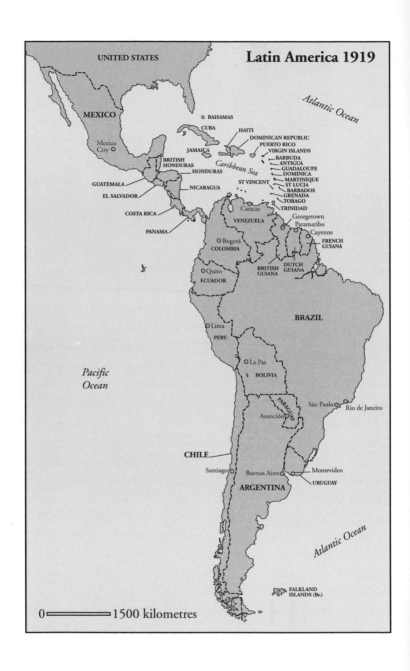

Latin America 1919

UNITED STATES

Atlantic Ocean

MEXICO

Mexico City ○

BAHAMAS

CUBA

HAITI

DOMINICAN REPUBLIC

PUERTO RICO

VIRGIN ISLANDS

JAMAICA

BRITISH HONDURAS

HONDURAS

GUATEMALA

EL SALVADOR

NICARAGUA

COSTA RICA

PANAMA

Caribbean Sea

BARBUDA

ANTIGUA

GUADALOUPE

DOMINICA

MARTINIQUE

ST VINCENT

ST LUCIA

BARBADOS

GRENADA

TOBAGO

TRINIDAD

Caracas ○

VENEZUELA

Georgetown

Paramaribo

Cayenne

FRENCH GUIANA

Bogotá ○

COLOMBIA

BRITISH GUIANA

DUTCH GUIANA

Quito ○

ECUADOR

BRAZIL

Lima ○

PERU

Pacific Ocean

La Paz ○

BOLIVIA

São Paulo ○

Rio de Janeiro ○

PARAGUAY

Asunción ○

CHILE

Santiago ○

Buenos Aires ○

Montevideo

URUGUAY

ARGENTINA

Atlantic Ocean

FALKLAND ISLANDS (Br.)

0 ══════ 1500 kilometres

Makers
of the
Modern
World

Central America and the Caribbean

Michael Streeter

HAUS HISTORIES

First published in Great Britain in 2010 by
Haus Publishing Ltd
70 Cadogan Place
London SW1X 9AH
www.hauspublishing.com

A CIP catalogue record for this book
is available from the British Library

ISBN 978-1-906598-25-9

Series design by Susan Buchanan
Typeset in Sabon by MacGuru Ltd
Printed in Dubai by Oriental Press

Contents

Preface

In 1890 the American naval officer and historian Alfred Thayer Mahan published a book that was to have a strong impact on the way that American leaders viewed their place in the world strategically and militarily. It was also to have a profound knock-on effect on the countries of Central America and the Caribbean. As its name suggests, *The Influence of Sea Power upon History* highlighted the importance of a powerful navy in a state's rise to power. Britain and the role of its Royal Navy were held up as a shining example of this.

To a country that was still absorbed in its own land-based expansion westwards, Mahan's emphasis on the role of the navy required a major shift in outlook for Washington, one it was nonetheless ultimately willing to adopt. But Mahan's influence did not end there. For decades, there had been talk in America about building a canal between the Atlantic and Pacific Oceans, via the isthmus, linking those two giant bodies of water. Such a route would have a major impact on trade routes, lessening reliance on the long and dangerous journey around Cape Horn. There had been considerable discussion about the possible location for such a crossing, with Panama and especially Nicaragua the most likely countries for it.

However, Mahan warned that the building of such a canal would change not just trade routes but the geopolitics of the entire region. In addition to the benefits it would bring, such a waterway could herald 'latent and yet unforeseen dangers to the peace of the western hemisphere'. Mahan noted, '... it is evident that ... this now comparatively deserted nook of the ocean will, like the Red Sea, become a great thoroughfare of shipping, and attract, as never before in our day, the interest and ambition of maritime nations.' He then warned that 'the United States is woefully unready ... to assert in the Caribbean and Central America a weight of influence proportioned to the extent of her interests'.[1]

In the following years leaders in Washington were to show vividly that they had taken these warnings to heart as they began to take far greater interest in the affairs of Central American and Caribbean states. This increased attention was to have a dramatic impact on the countries in that region. Not only would a number of them experience direct intervention by the United States and its troops, they would also find themselves catapulted onto the world stage; first, when war broke out in Europe, and then, secondly, during the subsequent attempts to broker the peace in Paris.

In September 1915 representatives of North, South and Central America met
to discuss the situation in Mexico. In 1919 some of them would meet again at
Versailles. On the left, Don Ignacio Calderon from Bolivia, in the foreground,
Don Joaquin Mendez from Guatemala and, second left, Robert L. Lansing the
US Secretary of State.

I

The Lives and the Land

1
Origins 1800–1900

The influence of geography upon history is always an important one. Nowhere is this truer than for the six Central American and Caribbean countries that were invited to take part in the Paris Peace Conference in 1919. The Central American states of Guatemala, Honduras, Nicaragua and Panama are on the narrow strip of land that joins the two land masses of North and South America. This places them strategically between the Atlantic and Pacific Oceans, a factor that has played a role in their development and history in the last 200 years. The island states of Haiti and Cuba, meanwhile, lie at the gateway between the Caribbean and the Atlantic. Between the two countries the stretch of water known as the Windward Passage is a major shipping route.

There is also another key factor that affects all six countries, which has been crucial not just in their modern history in general but specifically also in their involvement in the signing of the Treaty of Versailles. That crucial quirk of geography is their proximity to the United States of America. It is almost impossible to overstate the importance of the United States to the recent history of these six states. Their invitation to join in the Peace Conference, for example, was almost entirely due to the desire of Washington to have them present. This can be seen from the fact that another Central American state, Costa Rica, which had fulfilled precisely the same 'entry require-ment' for being at Paris as these six – joining the First World War on the Allies' side – was specifically excluded because the United States did not want it there. The story of these six small countries is thus intimately entwined with the foreign policy of the Great Power to the north.

Of the six, the four from Central America inevitably share many similarities in geography as well as history. Visitors to this isthmus have usually commented on its remarkable natural beauty, from its Pacific and Caribbean coastlines, many lakes, fertile lands, exotic flora and fauna to its plung-ing valleys. Linking all the region's countries from Guatemala in the north to Panama in the south is a range of volcanic mountains, adding different climatic and soil variety to the area. The abundance of life and fertility of the land, its stun-ning landscapes and the temperate climate of much of the highland interior, coupled with its strategic position, have long held out the prospect that the region would become a prosperous area that could rival other, larger regions of the world.

Yet there are geographical as well as more human reasons why Central America remains one of the poorer and, to a large extent, least developed parts of the world. The presence of its tall mountains, some of which reach as high as 14,000 feet, give a striking clue to one of the recurring obstacles to development in past centuries – volcanic eruptions and above all earthquakes. The region suffers from substantial tremors on a regular basis. In the 20th century destructive earthquakes occurred on average around once every two-and-a-half years.

In February 1976, for example, an earthquake measuring 7.5 on the Richter scale in Guatemala killed around 23,000 people and injured more than 75,000 others. The region is also regularly hit by hurricanes and suffers from torrential rain and mudslides, and on the Caribbean coast in particular has been plagued by a variety of tropical diseases. In addition, it lacks major navigable rivers and its remarkably few deep-water ports mean that communication both within the region and with the outside world has not always been easy.

Central America's location has, however, made it a meeting point of different cultures, from the north and south and also from the Caribbean. In pre-Conquest times the dominant culture was Mayan, which reached its peak around 600 AD to 900 AD. However, the Mayan culture had relatively little influence in the lands that are today Panama and Costa Rica. Moreover, even where Mayan culture was dominant, it was never centrally organised, such as is seen, for example, with the Aztecs in Mexico. Though they shared a common cultural identity, many Mayan communities lived in considerable autonomy. After the Conquest the population mix of the region contained Amerindians, whites – mostly from Spain – and mixed-race *ladinos* (the local word for *mestizos*).

Of the four Central American countries who sent delegates to Paris, the nation with the biggest indigenous influence is Guatemala, with Amerindians making up around 40 percent of the population. In Honduras, by contrast, *ladinos* and whites of European background make up 90 per cent of the population. In Nicaragua Amerindians make up just 5 per cent of the total population while in Panama that figure is 6 percent. Across the region there is also now a sizeable black population, either from slave populations brought in to work on plantations or descendants of freed or runaway slaves. In all of these countries the most widely spoken official tongue is Spanish, though in Guatemala in particular up to 40 per cent of people speak Amerindian languages.

Cuba, which is part of the Greater Antilles island group in the Caribbean, lies 90 miles south-west of Key West in Florida. The island stretches about 750 miles from its western tip near the Mexican mainland, to the eastern end which points towards the island of Hispaniola (Haiti and the Dominican Republic). Cuba is far less mountainous than Central America, consisting mostly of low rolling plains, apart from the Sierra Maestra range of mountains in the south-east of the country where the Pico Turquino reaches 6,466 feet (1,971 metres). It, too, is often hit by hurricanes. The original population of the island when it was visited, then conquered, by Europeans in the late 15th and early 16th century were the Ciboney and Taíno native Americans. However immigration from Europe – mostly Spain – and the importation of slaves from Africa to work the country's plantations means that for several 100 years the population has been a mixture of white, black and mixed race (*mulattos*). Its official and main language is Spanish.

Across the Windward Passage to the south-east, and also part of the Greater Antilles, is Haiti. This country occupies the western third of the island of Hispaniola; the rest of the island is the independent country of the Dominican Republic. A mountainous country, Haiti is noted for its beauty, even if its physical attractions are often overshadowed by its reputation for political turbulence. It, too, is hit by hurricanes, mudslides and, as was seen in January 2010, devastating earthquakes. Haiti is unique among the six Central American and Caribbean countries invited to Paris in not having a predominantly Spanish heritage. Before independence it was a French colony and to this day French remains one of its two official languages. The other is a French-based Creole, spoken mostly by the majority black population who were originally brought to the island as slaves; the minority mixed race (*mulattos*) and whites generally speak French. The original inhabitants of the island were the Taíno people who were all but wiped out by diseases brought to the island by Europeans. However some survived and eventually intermarried with runaway slaves on the island to create a defined mixed race group known as *zambos*.

There are significant differences between the modern histories of the six countries. For, while the four Central American states occupy the same stretch of land, they do not have a common past. The odd one out is Panama, which has a very different story from Honduras, Guatemala and Nicaragua. These last three were all part of what was known under Spanish rule as the Kingdom of Guatemala, which in turn was subject to the Viceroyalty of New Spain – Mexico today – as part of the Spanish Empire in the Americas. In practice the Kingdom enjoyed a considerable amount of autonomy from New Spain. Even among its constituent parts there were strong 'regional' identities in what would become Honduras, El Salvador, Nicaragua, Costa Rica and Guatemala. This may in part have been due to the fact that the pre-existing Mayan civilisation was decentralised; other factors that were certainly contributing causes were the political rivalries that grew up between the different areas and poor communications within the region generally.

The key events in the modern history of Honduras, Guatemala and Nicaragua occurred in the early 19th century, with the start of the revolutions that would eventually see most of South and Central America independent from Spain by the end of the third decade of that century. In much of South America the revolution was accompanied by bitter fighting and bloodshed. In Central America there was considerable unrest and discontent – many white Central Americans, or *creoles*, were unhappy about restrictions placed on them by Imperial Spain – but there was little real fighting. As would happen so often later in the region's affairs, events were dictated by events to the north; though in this case, it was Mexico rather than the United States that influenced the outcome. Mexico was going through its own independence birth pangs and Central Americans feared that its army would soon be heading south to 'free' the region from the Spanish. In order to avoid this undesirable form of help, the various regions of Central America jointly declared their own independence from Spain on 15 September 1821. The affair did not end there, however, as the new Mexican leader Agustín de Iturbide was busily creating a new empire. Rather than be forcibly annexed to this, a majority of Central American leaders agreed to join voluntarily with Mexico on 5 January 1822.

This subservience to Mexico did not last long, however. By early the following year Iturbide had abdicated, and on 1 July 1823 the Central Americans declared themselves fully independent, calling themselves the United Provinces of Central America. The only province to opt to stay with Mexico was Chiapas, which had formerly been part of the old Central American Kingdom. The new unified state consisted of Guatemala – the biggest and dominant partner, El Salvador, Honduras, Nicaragua and Costa Rica. It was a time of great optimism in the region, which had a total population of around 1.2 million people (65 percent of whom were Amerindian). A few years earlier, in 1815, no less a figure than the great Liberator of South America, Simón Bolívar, had predicted – or at least hoped for – great things for the 'states of the isthmus' when he declared: 'This magnificent location between the two great oceans could in time become the emporium of the world ... Perhaps some day the capital of the world may be located there, just as Constantine claimed Byzantium was the capital of the ancient world.'[1]

While few in Central America perhaps went so far as to share such lofty expectations for their backwater in 1823, there was nonetheless considerable optimism about the region's future based on its geographical location, the fertility of its soil and the opportunity it now finally had to join the world of international trade free from the restrictions of Imperial Spain.

Reality, however, soon set in. From the very birth of the United Provinces, Central American politics was beset by a political divergence that was to dominate – and rarely healthily – the region's politics for the rest of the century and well into the next. This was the bitter split between the Liberals and the Conservatives. In the ensuing decades it would not always be easy to distinguish between Liberals and Conservatives simply by their actions, as personal favouritism, corruption, abuse of power and dictatorships often tended to blur the lines of policy. Moreover both sets of politicians were generally drawn from the elites of societies, usually white/ *creole* in the case of the Conservatives with some *ladinos* among the Liberals. Yet there were important philosophical differences between them.

The Conservatives wanted to retain what they saw as the continuity and tradition of old Hispanic institutions, including the Church, and above all wanted stability and order and the maintenance of the ruling classes in power. The Liberals, meanwhile, were anti-clerical, opposed to what they considered excessive old 'Spanish' taxes, championed the abolition of slavery and determined to both modernise the country and boost trade. They also drew support from a slightly wider circle that included the professional classes, among whom were *ladinos* – though many would later turn against Liberal rule and policies. Crucially, the Liberals also supported the idea of a unified Central America, based on the one created in 1823. This was important because when the Liberals later lost power across the region, the idea of unity was jettisoned with them and remained out of favour for decades to come.

The main author of the downfall of the Liberals in Central America was himself a *ladino*. José Rafael Carrera was from the eastern mountains of Guatemala and has variously been described as a swineherd, bandit and peasant hero. He was certainly a shrewd military and political leader, and despite his modest background was to dominate the isthmus's politics for many years. Carrera led a revolt from his mountainous stronghold in 1837 and his ferocious peasants' army eventually seized power in Guatemala, the dominant part of the confederation of states. His main grievances, and those of many Conservatives, included recent judicial reforms, the anti-clerical measures brought in across the region, and a new 'head tax' – a tax per person – brought in by the Liberals. A serious outbreak of cholera and anti-Liberal preaching by Catholic priests added to the charged atmosphere across the region, and by 1840 Carrera had come to dominate not just Guatemala but also the other states of the United Provinces. The political clock was turned back, the Liberal reforms dismantled, education placed once more back in the hands of the Church and the head tax abolished to be replaced by the old tithe tax.

Carrera was to have a decisive influence not just on

Guatemala but all the Central American states until his death in 1865. A classic *caudillo* or military ruler, his was an authoritarian rule and he demanded the complete obedience of his followers. His reaction on seeing a portrait of Napoleon Bonaparte – 'another me' he is said to have exclaimed[2] – gives a clue as to this ill-educated but astute strongman's approach to power. His ascendancy kept the Liberals out of power for nearly three decades and also brought a swift end to one of the Liberals' cherished policies – that of a united Central America. From the moment in July 1838 that the Federal Congress of the United Provinces decreed that the constituent states were sovereign, free and independent, the Bolivarian dream of unity in the isthmus was shattered forever. Attempts would later be made to revive the idea by various successors of the Liberal mantle, but the differences and growing national identity of each country would ultimately prove too great. From now on Guatemala, Honduras and Nicaragua – as well as Costa Rica and El Salvador – would remain sovereign independent states.

One feature of this devolution into separate states was the number of disputes that occurred between neighbours in this period, contributing to the instability of the region. Another was the way sovereignty would be threatened by outside forces, not just throughout the rest of the 19th century but for the majority of the 20th century as well. Though Central America's strategically important position between the two great oceans had not brought it great riches – the countries produced modest exports at the time, such as cochineal from Guatemala – the European powers and the United States had shown growing interest in the region because of its geographical importance. In particular, rivalry was growing between the traditional foreign power in the region, Great Britain, and the emerging power to the north of the United States. The self-serving and often destructive nature of this interest was perfectly demonstrated in what became known as the William Walker Affair.

William Walker was an intelligent, charismatic man from Tennessee who had flirted with careers in medicine, the law and journalism in the 1840s before turning his attention to life as an adventurer. His chosen target was Nicaragua, which had long been considered the best potential place for a trans-isthmus canal because of its lakes and river systems. The canal issue had become the subject of complex wrangling between both Liberals and Conservatives inside the country and Britain and United States outside. The Liberals had lost power in Nicaragua and appealed for help from American sources. The outcome was that Walker and 57 others travelled down to Central America in June 1855 to attempt to take power in Nicaragua on the Liberals' behalf.

Walker soon seized control of the country, and an appeal for volunteers saw more than 2,500 men from the southern United States – many of them veterans of the Mexican War a few years earlier – travel south to Central America. Thanks to his support from the Liberals, Walker was able to offer large land concessions to these volunteers from the American Deep South. In 1856 Walker decreed English to be the country's official language, tried to force peasants to work for large landowners and legalised slavery. There was fear that the entire region was at threat from both Walker and the United States, which had recognised the adventurer's regime. This alarm was not just felt by Conservative politicians among the region's countries but by Britain, too, which was worried about losing influence over trade and any potential canal route to its rivals in Washington. The British began a naval blockade that stopped Walker from gaining additional reinforcements while troops from the other Central American States took part in what became known as the National War against Walker's motley followers.

Eventually, worn down by battle and disease, most of Walker's men deserted and returned home; and after the United States intervened to broker a truce, the adventurer himself surrendered and was taken back to the United States aboard one of his country's warships. Back in New Orleans Walker was acclaimed a hero and was soon attempting a second expedition to Central America, though he was thwarted by the United States Navy. His third and final foray took him to the Bay Islands off Honduras, from where Walker harboured dreams of reuniting the nations of the isthmus. However, by now his support had dwindled and the 'grey-eyed man of destiny', as he was known, was captured by British troops and handed over to the Honduran authorities. They put him on trial and executed him in 1860. Though he had achieved nothing and had left death and chaos in his wake, there was something of the tragi-comic about Walker. More importantly, his abortive interventions in the region were a foretaste of what was to come on a much bigger and more organised scale later. It also set nations in the isthmus on their guard against the United States, a country that until the middle of the century had not shown great interest in the region.

The Liberals' initial support for Walker in Nicaragua set back their political cause across the region. Yet by the 1860s there was a mood of political change across Latin America, including in Central America. The era of the Conservative *caudillos* was coming to an end, as business and commercial interests became frustrated by the lack of economic progress and trade in the region, and at the lack of vision of many of the resolutely inward-looking and cliquey leaders. Instead a new breed of Liberals was emerging: younger men whose ideas were influenced by one of the dominant trends in Latin American political thought at this time, positivism. In essence this meant an emphasis on order and progress, and the use of technological solutions and education to modernise the country, its structures and its economy. Traditional Liberal emphasis on freedom gave way to a more pragmatic approach to solutions, in which lofty ideals might have to wait until the country and its institutions could develop economically and financially.

Of key importance to this new breed of Liberals in Central American society was overseas trade; in particular the export of raw materials and the import of manufactured goods from industrial countries. To achieve these aims a country needed good transport systems – this was an era of the construction of railways, roads and ports – and of course the right crops to export. For the second half of the 19th century this meant coffee.

Costa Rica had begun to develop its coffee production in the 1830s, but it was not until later in the century that Guatemala, Honduras and Nicaragua followed the same path. However, growing coffee proved so popular and profitable with landowners that by 1870 it had become Guatemala's largest export crop. It dominated the market in Nicaragua too, though the industry was less important in Honduras in this period. The market for coffee was overwhelmingly the United States, Britain, Germany and France. As much of the land as well as production remained in local hands, these countries thus enjoyed considerable economic clout within Central America. In Guatemala, in particular, coffee exporters became very reliant on Germany, which by the early 20th century imported more from that country than all the other major Western nations combined.

The new Liberal era in Central America did not mean the end of strong authoritarian leaders. The demands of 'order and progress' meant that there had to be a strong leader. This was an era of what might be termed 'republican dictators' who controlled national elections and institutions, and who usually sought to stay in power until they were forcibly ejected. The military also began to play an increasingly important role in political life, often as self-appointed arbiters as to who should be in power. Corruption and brutality among the ruling elites were never far away in this period.

In Guatemala two key dictators were Justo Rufino Barrios, who ruled for twelve years until 1885, and Manuel Estrada Cabrera, whose reign at the top lasted for twenty-two years from 1898. In Nicaragua, where the revival of Liberal fortunes had been delayed by the Walker affair, Liberalism took longer to establish itself. But the archetypal 'republican dictator' there was José Santos Zelaya, a tough leader who was to make himself very unpopular with the United States. Meanwhile in Honduras the last decade of the century saw a Zelaya protégé take power – Policarpo Bonilla, the man who would later sign the Treaty of Versailles on his country's behalf.

José Policarpo Bonilla Vásquez was born in Tegucigalpa in Honduras on 17 March 1858, the son of Inocete Bonilla, a lawyer originally from Nicaragua, and Juana Vásquez. Bonilla was blessed with both intelligence and a strong personality, and after studying philosophy he followed in his father's footsteps to become a lawyer. Later he travelled to the United States and also founded a law firm, Fortín & Bonilla. However by then he had developed a taste for politics, and by 1880 was a deputy in the country's national congress. Three

years later a still youthful Bonilla was governor of Tegucigalpa, and he also served under the government of Honduran dictator Marco Aurelio Soto, as well as creating his own
newspaper *El Bien Publico* in 1890. In 1891 Bonilla, who was
a fine orator, harboured presidential ambitions of his own
and unsuccessfully stood against Ponciano Leiva, an old
soldier who had been President once before back in the 1870s.

These were politically charged times inside Honduras,
which also enjoyed tense relations with neighbouring Nicaragua. After Bonilla lost the 1891 election he was accused
of conspiring to seize power and fled to Nicaragua where he
began to plot his return. He organised an attempted invasion of Honduras in 1893 that led to Leiva's downfall, but
the presidency passed instead to General Domingo Vásquez,
whose forces repelled the invasion. Bonilla was not to be so
easily thwarted in his ambition, however. Enlisting the military backing of Nicaragua – where his mentor Zelaya was in
power – Bonilla launched another assault on Honduras. In
February 1894 Vásquez was forced to quit the capital Tegucigalpa. The fighting continued for some months in the country,
but the invader had got what he wanted. Bonilla's energy had
finally been rewarded with the presidency.

Bonilla's plotting was not just confined to politics. An
intriguing glimpse into his character comes in a story about
how he fell out with namesake General Manuel Bonilla, who
in 1893 had been a trusted supporter. It is said that the two
men were courting two sisters of a well-to-do Honduran
family that was inordinately proud of its European heritage. Policarpo Bonilla was, like that family, of pure-blooded
white Spanish stock. But Manuel Bonilla was a mixed-race
ladino, and when Policarpo discreetly let slip to the two
sisters' family details about his namesake's mixed heritage

they promptly broke off relations with him.[3] A perhaps more plausible explanation for their growing enmity was more political; Manuel Bonilla was a strong supporter of foreign trade links and investment, while Policarpo Bonilla, though a Liberal, had developed a dislike for the influence of foreign countries and companies on Honduras. This was a trait he had picked up from his mentor Zelaya.

In power, Bonilla displayed his concern over American influence by passing a land law that, in theory at least, prevented foreign firms from buying up vast tracts of land. In one sense, Bonilla's antipathy towards foreign powers was curious, given that as a lawyer he had worked for American mining interests, apparently with no qualms. However there was a more personal reason for his attitude towards Americans, as well as the principled one. When Vásquez was fighting against Bonilla, the veteran general had employed a number of sharpshooters – including many from the United States.

Though Bonilla was less open than some to deals with foreign firms, in other ways he was certainly true to the Liberal traditions of the region and Honduras – for example in his support for the idea of a united Central America. Since its demise nearly sixty years earlier, reuniting the constituent nations into one larger and more powerful nation had remained just a dream. However, with men such as Zelaya and Bonilla in power in the 1890s the dream became, briefly, a reality. For Bonilla the purpose of such a union was to protect the region from outside interference. In 1895 the British Navy had blockaded a Nicaraguan port following a dispute between the countries. Britain eventually relented after intervention by the United States, but for Bonilla it was too good an opportunity to be missed. He invited his counterparts from Nicaragua and El Salvador to a meeting in Amapala in

Honduras where on 20 June 1895 the three leaders signed an agreement to create the Greater Republic of Central America. It was a bold move and briefly seemed capable of surviving when the United States appeared to back the move. However, in 1896 Washington changed tack and refused to recognise the new 'nation's' ambassador and two years later the new unified state had collapsed. The following year Bonilla left office and went to live abroad as the new century dawned. Despite an anti-climatic end to his presidency, his attempts to reform the country, notably its civil code, and protect it from foreign influence earned him praise in some quarters. The historian and writer Rafael Heliodoro Valle later said of him that Bonilla was a 'hero' who had given the country 'a new conscience'.[4]

Nicaragua's delegate at the Paris Peace Conference was never himself President of his country, but there was no shortage of them in his family. Salvador Chamorro Oreamuno was a member of one of his country's best known political families, and grew up in the middle of the century during the turmoil of the Walker Affair in Nicaragua. His uncle, Pedro Joaquín Chamorro Alfaro, had been President of Nicaragua for four years from 1875, and had earlier been involved in the struggle against William Walker, while his own brother Rosendo would briefly be President in 1923. Salvador Chamorro was from Granada in Nicaragua, a bastion of the Conservatives. Here he met Gregoria Vargas Báez and produced a son Emiliano Chamorro – born in Acoyapa in 1871 – who would twice be President of the country in the 20th century. It was he who chose his father to be Nicaragua's delegate at the Paris Peace Conference. However according to Emiliano's autobiography he did not know he was the son of Salvador Chamorro until he was aged fourteen; until then he thought his father was a man called Evaristo Enríquez. Indeed, Salvador Chamorro seems to have had a complicated private life. For example, a relationship with Rita Montenegro, also from Granada, produced a daughter, Carlota Chamorro Montenegro. In keeping with family tradition, Salvador Chamorro was involved in politics and later became President of the country's Chamber of Deputies. But he also had a keen interest in business, and in October 1892 was one of the founder members of Nicaragua's first Chamber of Commerce. Guatemala's future delegate in Paris, Joaquín Méndez, was from a similar generation to Salvador Chamorro, born in 1861. By profession Méndez was a journalist, but he would later turn to politics – he was deputy in his country's parliament for San Juan Sacatepéquez – and serve as a government minister, ultimately becoming a highly successful diplomat.

While Guatemala, Honduras and Nicaragua had achieved independence early in the 19th century, their near neighbour in Central America, Panama, did not share a similar fate. Unlike the other three, Panama had not been part of New Spain under Spanish rule but had been part first of Peru and then the Viceroyalty of New Granada, which included what is now Colombia. New Granada became independent of Spain in 1819, though because of its physical separation from Panama, the latter technically remained under Spanish rule until 1821. It was then rejoined to Colombia under the accepted doctrine that newly independent nations kept the territories that they had administered in colonial times. So while independent of Spain in the 19th century, Panama remained under the control of the South American country. But though Panama was historically part of Colombia, geographically it was part of Central America and is separated from South America by the Darién Gap, an area of thick impenetrable forest and swamps. This physical barrier added to the Panamanian sense that it was different from Colombia, and during the 19th century a growing independence movement developed. Briefly in 1830 and 1831 and then for more than a year from 1840 Panama enjoyed independence, and for much of the century its citizens were largely left to govern their own affairs. However it would not be until the 20th century that full and lasting Panamanian independence would occur, and, as will be seen in the following chapter, this event owed as much to United States ambitions in the region and internal Colombian turmoil as to Panamanian nationalism.

Its future delegate in Paris, Antonio Burgos, a career diplomat born in Chitré, the capital of the Panamanian province of Herrera, in February 1873, would have to wait until he was in his early thirties before his country saw independence. The son of José Burgos and Maria de la Cruz Rodriguez, Burgos had a varied education, attending the University of Cartagena in Colombia and studying philosophy, the arts and science. This eclectic education was to be reflected in the astonishing breadth of subjects on which he would write books in later years, ranging from child psychology to immigration and from ancient history to geography. He also pursued a career in politics and was a deputy in Panama's Legislative Assembly (while it was still part of Colombia) and civil and military governor of Colón. Later, however, like Méndez in Guatemala, Burgos would carve out a career as a diplomat.

Though Cuba is a Caribbean rather than Central American country, its move towards independence shared similarities with that of Panama. Like the Central American country, the Spanish-American revolutions of the second two decades of the 19th century did not leave the Caribbean island independent. For one thing, Cuba was a hard place for external forces to attack, and Spain was determined to cling on to this precious part of its Empire. More importantly, there was at this time little appetite among the largely white aristocracy on the island for change. The island's economy was dominated by sugar plantations worked by African slaves – by 1860 the island supplied a third of the world's sugar – and fresh supplies of new slaves depended on Spanish rule. Moreover, as we shall see shortly, the recent example of Haiti had shown the ruling classes the dangers – for them – of encouraging ideas of freedom and liberation. However irksome Spanish rule was for the local elites – and it was – it was deemed preferable to bloody insurrection.

Cuba, then, remained in Spanish hands until almost the very end of the century. Yet there was during the course of the decades a growing independence movement on the island. This reached a climax in 1868 with the start of what became known as the Ten Years War. Local elites, including plantation owners increasingly unhappy with rule from Madrid, took up arms against the Spanish who still had a grip on the wealth created by the island's sugar economy. It was a bloody and brutal conflict, with the Spanish slowly but relentlessly wiping out opposition. Divisions among the local elites or *creoles* and concern over the likely role of the black majority in an independent Cuba were contributing factors in the nationalists' defeat. By 1878 the struggle was effectively over, despite a further outbreak of fighting at the end of that decade.

The decisive move towards independence came in 1895 when veterans of the Ten Years War launched another offensive. They used what by now were the well-worn tactics of Cuban revolutionaries, which were to sail men and munitions from the United States mainland, disembark in the south-east corner furthest away from the capital Havana, and then vanish into the peaks of the Sierra Maestra. One of those landing in 1895 was José Martí.

As the war developed in Cuba, across the Straits of Florida people were showing a close interest in events. There was a growing clamour in the United States for intervention on behalf of the Cuban nationalists and against the Spanish imperialists. Essentially there were three motivations for this. One was a genuine desire on the part of many Americans to aid Cubans as the popular press whipped up anti-Spanish feeling with tales of atrocities. This was a war in which the press played a major role in shaping public and political opinion. A second key reason was Cuba's strategic position as the gateway to the Central American isthmus, and its location so close to American soil. A third reason was the lucrative sugar industry on the island, where American capital was playing a growing role. 'It makes the water come to my mouth when I think of the State of Cuba as one in our family,' an American financier observed in 1895.[5]

José Martí (1853–1895) was a revered figure in the Cuban independence movement both during his lifetime and after his death. A poet, lawyer and journalist, after the abortive revolution ended in 1878 he lived in exile in the United States, where he worked as a journalist, and in various Latin American cities, and became one of the most eloquent voices for the nationalist cause. He took part in the attempted revolution in 1895 that was to lead to the Spanish-American War and the end of Spanish rule. He was killed by Spanish troops in May 1895 but remained a key figure for nationalists.

Not everyone was keen to get involved in the conflict. President William McKinley, for one, was reluctant for the United States to intervene. However, in April 1898 the USS *Maine*, an American ship that had been sent to Havana to help safeguard American citizens, exploded in that city's harbour. To this day there is still mystery surrounding the exact causes of the blast, even after four investigations. However the incident was made the most of by the popular press, led by newspaper baron William Randolph Hearst, who insisted the Spanish were to blame. The US Congress voted to declare war. Thanks to the superiority of American forces, the fighting did not last long in what was famously described by future President Theodore Roosevelt, who led his own regiment in the conflict, as a 'splendid little war'. By August the war was over and later that same year Cuba formally became independent of Spain. The United States also took control of the Spanish possessions of Puerto Rico, Guam and the Philippines as a result of the war. It was a conflict that marked the final end of the Spanish Empire and the start of a new era of United States expansionism. In Cuba itself, however, the nationalists could have forgiven themselves for thinking that their cause had been rather overlooked in the conflict. Their own army was quickly dismantled by the United States, as the island was occupied by American troops. It was hardly the most promising of starts for Cuban independence.

Looking on at events in his home country was Antonio Sánchez de Bustamante y Sirvén. Born on 13 April 1865, Bustamante, the son of Juan Manuel Sánchez de Bustamante y Garcia del Barrio and Dolores Sirvén y Borras, had by this time already established a reputation as an outstanding lawyer, a reputation that would help earn him the post as Cuba's delegate in Paris in 1919. Intriguingly there is some evidence that at the start of the Cuban nationalist uprising in 1895 his sympathies may have lain with Spain rather than the nationalists. An open letter in 1896 addressed to the Spanish Captain General of Cuba General Valeriano Weyler pledged the signatories' support for him and bitterly attacked the 'slanders' of the Spanish official made in the United States Congress. The authors pledged their loyalty to the Spanish flag and promised to 'sustain and maintain it, our lives and our fortunes'. One of those who signed was A.S. de Busta-mante. [6] As a young man, Bustamante had studied in both Havana and Madrid – perhaps a clue to his Spanish sympathies, if sympathies they were – and by 1886 was already a Doctor of Civil, Canon and Administrative Law.

By the time Cuba finally achieved independence – of a sort – its close neighbour across the Windward Passage had already been a separate state for nearly a century. Though the entire island of Hispaniola had been under Spanish control in the first part of the 17th century, the western third of the island was formally controlled by France following a treaty with Spain in 1697 and named Saint-Domingue. Haiti thus had a French rather than a Spanish heritage. The impact of the 1789 Revolution in France was inevitably felt on the Caribbean island. A revolt by slaves ensued, and the former slave Toussaint L'Ouverture became the state's military leader. He was later captured by the French and taken to Europe, where he died in jail of pneumonia in 1803. However one of his lieutenants, Jean-Jacques Dessalines, continued the struggle and the newly named Haiti – a local name for the island – was proclaimed an independent state in 1804. It was the first post-colonial independent black nation in the world.

> Old Man Brown is more divine, I believe
> Only love can accompany this prodigy!
>
> **TERTULIEN GUILBAUD ON ABOLITIONIST JOHN BROWN**

Independence was not easy for Haiti in the 19th century. The revolutionary wars had left the sugar industry badly disrupted, and the breakup of the large plantations led to less

efficiency and use of modern techniques than found in countries such as Cuba. The country was also affected by internal
racial tensions between the minority French-speaking light-
skinned mulattos and the mostly Creole-speaking majority black population. The country also had to cope with
the antipathy of more powerful countries: France imposed
financial penalties on Haiti while the United States, which
had its own sizeable population of black slaves, did not
formally recognise the country's independence until 1862.
Germany and Spain, too, meddled in the island's affairs. As
the century came to its close the instability on the island grew,
while American commentators and journalists painted a grim
picture of life in the country.

It was during this difficult period that the country's future
delegate Tertulien Guilbaud grew up. Born in Port-de-Paix in
May 1856, Guilbaud was the son of a black Haitian father
and a mulatto mother. He studied at lycées or French sec-
ondary schools in first *Cap-Haïtien* and then Port-au-Prince,
winning a prize for philosophy at the age of eighteen, before
teaching himself, first literature and then mathematics. He
then became a schools inspector and later travelled overseas to
study law at the University of Paris. When Guilbaud returned
to Haiti in 1888 he practised as a lawyer and then worked as
a senior schools inspector before founding the law school, the
École libre de Droit du *Cap-Haïtien*, which formally opened
in 1893. For a year Guilbaud gave all the lectures himself,
before calling upon the services of two former classmates
from his Paris days to teach there. Guilbaud had also entered
politics, and was a member of the Constituent Assembly that
drew up a new constitution for the country in 1889.

By then Guilbaud had already carved out a reputation as
a writer, his prose influenced by Victor Hugo. As a poet his

main theme was patriotism and his most famous collection, published in 1885, was called *Patrie*, or Fatherland. This collection earned him the title of 'national poet'. In one of the poems 'John Brown' Guilbaud compares the white abolitionist who was hanged in Virginia for his anti-slavery actions to Toussaint L'Ouverture. Pointing out that Brown was white and chose to die for his cause of helping black people, Guilbaud noted, 'Old Man Brown is more divine, I believe ... Oh! Only love can accompany this prodigy!'[7]

By the end of the 19th century Guilbaud's beloved Haiti had at least managed to maintain her sovereignty and independence despite the internal tensions and external pressures. But as the United States' regional ambitions grew, this was not a situation that would survive long into the next century. In Central America and the Caribbean, the early part of the 20th century would belong to Washington.

2
The Age of Interventions 1900–1914

The American intervention in Cuba at the end of the 19th century was a striking example of how the United States' policy towards its near-neighbours in Central America and the Caribbean was changing. Growing commercial interest in the region, its vital strategic importance and the more nebulous but important notion of 'manifest destiny' – the idea that the new nation of the United States was destined to expand not just from the Atlantic to the Pacific but into neighbouring regions too – all played their part. Nowhere was this growing ambition more evident than in Panama and the ultimate creation of the Panama Canal in the early 20th century.

The idea of a direct shipping route between the two great oceans was nothing new. Various schemes to build a canal across the isthmus went back as far as the 17th century. Though it represents the shortest route, many of the plans did not focus on Panama – though an important railway route across it connecting the oceans was completed in 1855 – but rather on Nicaragua, because of its natural river and lake system. In particular, American interest was focused more on Nicaragua than Panama initially, and as late as the 1890s this was still the preferred option for US engineers.

By that time the United States had become convinced that a canal across the isthmus was not just desirable but absolutely essential. In part this was because of the influential book by the historian Alfred Thayer Mahan. In his *The Influence of Sea Power upon History*, Mahan insisted on the crucial importance of a strong navy. For the United States, which in the second half of the 19th century had aggressively expanded westwards to the Pacific coast, this meant having a fleet that could operate between both oceans. Hence the conviction in the country's Department of the Navy that a canal allowing easy transit from one body of water to the other was in the national interest. In the 1890s Theodore Roosevelt served as Assistant Secretary of the Navy and became personally convinced of this. So when he became President in 1901 it was little surprise that getting a canal built was high on his foreign policy agenda.

There were, though, a few obstacles to getting the canal constructed. One was the technical challenge, although the French company that had built the Suez Canal (the first French Canal Company – La Société International du Canal Interocéanique) was confident it could build one across Panama, even if it lacked the capital to carry it out. Another obstacle was national sovereignty. Though late in the 19th century many in the United States still favoured the Nicaraguan route, the government in Nicaragua was by no means fully pliable. Its nationalistic dictator José Zelaya made clear he would not simply hand over rights of sovereignty in relation to the canal and its surrounding land. His stance made building a canal there politically risky, as well as ensuring the Nicaraguan leader the lasting enmity of Washington. The chief engineer of the French canal project, Philippe Bunau-Varilla, had

PANAMA CANAL AND THE CANAL ZONE

The original rights to build a canal through Panama were owned by a French company, La Société International du Canal Interocéanique, and work began on it in 1880. However financial and technical problems and the crippling effect of disease (mostly yellow fever and malaria) among the workforce – more than 21,000 died – led to the project being abandoned. The United States bought the rights to construction from the French firm for $40 million, and after its treaty with the newly independent Panama in 1903 began work on it in 1904. The 50-mile canal had locks to regulate the water levels at both the Atlantic and Pacific ends.

As well as the engineering feat involved, one of the major challenges was to control and eradicate the disease that had so ravaged the French effort to build the canal. The Americans greatly improved sanitation and hygiene, but even so, 5,609 people perished during the building of the canal from 1904 to 1914. The ability for the Americans to have control over sanitation was to be a key issue in subsequent negotiations with Panama on the status of the Canal Zone. The canal opened in August 1914, two years ahead of schedule, and cost around $375 million.

The Canal Zone itself extended about five miles either side of the waterway. Under the terms of the original treaty, the area was run by the Canal Zone Government headed by a governor and was an 'unincorporated territory' of the United States. Thousands of American servicemen and women and civilians lived in the Canal Zone, which was in effect a medium-sized American town located in the middle of the isthmus. The limited rights of Panama regarding the Zone and issues such as competition from American businesses and tariffs were to remain sources of tension between the Central American state and Washington, and led to subsequent amendments of the original 1903 treaty. Full sovereignty and control of the canal finally passed to Panama at the end of 1999.

meanwhile been helping persuade Americans that Panama was the best location for the project, and by the time he came to power Roosevelt had come round to this view himself. There was still one last obstacle, however: the reluctance of the Colombians to allow the United States sovereignty over the Canal Zone (the land surrounding the proposed water-way itself).

Colombia was in turmoil at the turn of the century, involved in the middle of a bitter civil war. In relation to Panama, mean-while, there was strong nationalist feeling against handing the French company's existing canal concession to the United States and giving the Americans sovereignty over the pro-posed Canal Zone. However the Colombian authorities were in a difficult position. If they proved too awkward to deal with, they risked the United States opting for the Nicaraguan route, which would mean losing the chance to generate the substantial income that a canal concession in Panama could bring. After all, there was only likely to be one canal through the isthmus, at least for the foreseeable future. To compli-cate matters further, the United States had landed troops on Panamanian soil to quell disturbances there, without the prior knowledge of the Colombian authorities. Ultimately, American and Colombian diplomats agreed a treaty – the Hay-Herrán Treaty – in January 1903 that gave Washington the right to build a canal with a 10-mile wide zone around it. The United States would have the right to protect both law and order and health there, but Colombia would retain ultimate sovereignty.

The Colombian Congress, however, refused to ratify the agreement, and events then took a dramatic turn. The French engineer Bunau-Varilla, working with Panamanian politi-cian Manuel Amador, began plotting a nationalist uprising in Panama. There seems little doubt that Roosevelt was at the very least aware of the plot at an early stage, but did nothing to discourage it. Indeed by 2 November 1903 American war-ships were already steaming their way to Panama to ensure that Colombian troops could not arrive in time to quash the revolt. On 6 November the United States hastily recognised the new Republic of Panama while Bunau-Varilla, who was still a French citizen, had installed himself as the new country's representative in Washington. On 18 November he agreed a treaty on behalf of his new country that gave the United States the right to build the canal, and also handed over far more control of the proposed Canal Zone than the original agreement with Colombia would have done. This was signed and sent off to Panama by Bunau-Varilla before a Panamanian delegation despatched to negotiate the concession could even reach Washington. Nonetheless, anxious to please their powerful ally, the Panamanian authorities agreed to the controversial treaty.

Work soon began on canal construction, and by 1914 the 50-mile canal was complete. For the United States it was the perfect outcome, as it now held effective sovereignty over the Canal Zone. Roosevelt certainly showed little regret at his role in the way that his administration 'took the Canal Zone', as he put it. Indeed he took full responsibility for it. 'The vital work, getting Panama as an independent republic, on which all else hinged, was done by me without the aid or advice of anyone, save in so far as they carried out my instructions; and without the knowledge of anyone,' he wrote.[1] As for Panama, its people had gained independence but at a price: the indefinite presence of American personnel right across the heart of the country. Meanwhile, for Antonio Burgos, who had been a signatory of the new country's constitution, his domestic political career was about to end. He travelled to Genoa to be Panama's Consul General in Italy before, in 1913, heading to Madrid to be his nation's Minister there.

It is hard not to draw a parallel between the circumstances surrounding the independence of Panama and that of Cuba.

In both cases it was achieved with the direct intervention of the United States, ensuring that sovereignty would be, in practice, limited from the start. In the case of Cuba, independence started with the boots of American soldiers trampling on its soil. The United States rapidly disbanded the nationalist army that had fought against the Spanish, ensuring that the rebels could not later turn their fire upon the American occupiers. Meanwhile a convention was set up among elected officials to draw up a new constitution for the country. In theory this last move was a guarantee of Cuban self-determination. In practice the Americans had their own conditions they wished to impose on Cuba's future rulers – and this was in the form of what was called the Platt Amendment.

Washington was determined that this amendment, named after a US Senator, was to be inserted into the Cuban constitution. Its purpose was to give the United States the right to intervene directly in the island to preserve its independence or to ensure that its government was able to protect life and property. It also established the right of the United States to establish naval bases there. The existing American base at Guantánamo Bay dates from this agreement.

For Washington it was a safeguard against lawlessness on the island – crucial for business interests – and against foreign intervention. But nationalists realised that this measure would make Cuba a protectorate of the United States, and initially the convention officials were opposed to it. However, after assurances from US Secretary of War Elihu Root that the amendment did not compromise Cuba's sovereignty, the convention finally agreed to it in December 1901. The Platt Amendment was to remain in force for three decades.

On 20 May 1902 the country's new President was inaugurated. Tomás Estrada Palma was from a distinguished family and had been a wealthy landowner. During the Ten Years War he had been imprisoned by the Spanish and later went to live in the United States, where he worked as a teacher. His record of opposition to the Spanish and a reputation for honesty made him a popular candidate with most Cubans. But to the satisfaction of Washington he was also solidly pro-American.

The acclaimed Nicaraguan poet Rubén Darío was not alone in looking upon the United States' treatment of Cuba with disquiet. He wondered what José Martí would have said about seeing how 'under cover of aid to the grief-stricken pearl of the West Indies, the "monster" gobbles it up, oyster and all'. In fact Martí would probably not have been surprised. Not long before his death the nationalist said that his duty was not just to overthrow Spanish rule but also to 'prevent the United States with the independence of Cuba extending itself through the West Indies and falling with added weight upon our lands of America'. [2]

Cuba's new status did at least give Antonio Sánchez de Bustamante the chance to launch a political career of his own, and he served as a senator from 1902 to 1918. However it was in international law that the lawyer really excelled, and he was chosen as the head of Cuba's delegation for the second Hague Conference in 1907.

The United States' growing list of interventions in Central America and the Caribbean was inevitably causing disquiet not just in the region itself but in the diplomatic corridors of other major powers around the world. To many observers in Latin America, Washington's actions seemed little more than naked opportunism and expansionism. President Teddy Roosevelt, however, sought to justify his country's actions in the context of the famous Monroe Doctrine that dated from the 19th century.

In 1904 Roosevelt extended the doctrine, pointing out that if it wanted to avoid European intervention in Central America and the Caribbean, the United States might need to intervene itself to bring order to failing states. This meant not just those countries in a state of lawlessness but any that were unable to meet their international financial obligations; in essence, repay their debts. To many horrified observers in the region the Roosevelt Corollary, as it became known, effectively gave the Americans *carte blanche* to intervene where and when they liked.

The Monroe Doctrine was articulated by US President James Monroe in 1823 and was in essence a warning to European powers not to meddle or intervene in the Americas. In return the United States would stay out of European affairs. In theory this gave the newly independent nations of South and Central America protection against nations from the Old World. By the end of the 19th century, however, it was seen by many in South and Central America – and in the United States too – as justifying Washington's expansion in the region.

Though the Corollary was undoubtedly a self-serving and – to many – iniquitous doctrine, there were nonetheless some legitimate grounds for concern about the threat from European powers in the region. Roosevelt's declaration had followed the so-called Venezuela Affair of 1902 when British and German warships blockaded that country, claiming it had threatened British citizens and shown a complete lack of willingness to pay off long-standing foreign debts. The blockade caused deep unease in the United States and outrage throughout Latin America. Roosevelt himself protested against the blockade, and after lengthy international diplomacy the issue was resolved. However Roosevelt was determined that such an episode should not occur again so close to the United States.

The affair highlighted growing concern in the United States and the region, not just about European powers in general, but about the intentions of Germany in particular. This was a period in which Berlin was flexing its muscles economically, diplomatically and militarily around the world, aware that it lacked the global reach and possessions of its main European rivals, Britain and France. A considerable part of the Guatemalan coffee industry was already under the control of German business interests. A German firm owned and equipped the electricity generating plant in Guatemala City and Germany was also the leading commercial nation in terms of volume of exports there, though this was the only country in Latin America in which this was the case. Economically, Germany had influence across the isthmus, too; by 1913 it accounted for 21 percent of all trade with the Central American republics, more than Britain.

Nor was the Venezuela Affair the only time Germany used force to attempt to bully countries in Latin America and the Caribbean into submission. As long ago as 1872 the Germans had sent two warships, the *Vineta* and the *Gazella*, to Haiti to persuade its government to pay compensation to Germans whose businesses there had suffered losses because of unrest on the island. In December 1897 the Haitian government was humiliated over the case of a Haitian citizen of German origin called Emil Luders who had been – so Berlin believed – wrongly imprisoned. Luders was later allowed to leave the country, but this was not enough for Germany. It sent two warships into Port-au-Prince harbour and their commanders threatened to bombard the city unless Haiti gave a formal apology, arranged for a 21-gun salute of the German flag, paid compensation and allowed Luders to return to the country. Haiti gave in, to the chagrin of many nationalists on the island.

In 1902 Germany intervened militarily yet again, taking

the side of one faction as rival politicians bid for control of Haiti. This was when a Haitian naval commander, Admiral Hamilton Killick, a nationalist who supported the other faction in the power struggle and who opposed foreign intervention, showed extraordinary devotion to his cause after a German ship tried to capture his vessel. Rather than yielding to the German ship, he ordered everyone off his vessel, wrapped himself in the Haitian flag and then blew up his ship and himself with it.

The United States certainly seems to have feared German intentions in the Caribbean. According to Secretary of War Root, an 'important consideration' in explaining why Washington was so insistent on the Platt Amendment in Cuba was its 'suspicions' over possible German designs in the region.[3] Diplomatically, too, Germany exerted considerable influence. Concern about German influence in the region grew after the 1910 revolution in Mexico, which saw that country's relations with the United States deteriorate and thus it become a potential ally for another foreign power such as Germany. This concern would come to play a part in the politics of the Central American and Caribbean states in the First World War and also in the subsequent invitation of the six countries to the Paris Peace Conference.

Nonetheless, in pre-First World War Central America the biggest fear was over North American rather than potential German intervention. In 1905, for example, the United States took over the administration of the ailing Dominican Republic's customs duties – a major source of revenue for the state. This was an explicit application of the Roosevelt Corollary, as Washington agreed to use part of the income to pay off the republic's massive foreign debt, thus intending to prevent any chance of creditors arriving there armed with warships.

THE MEXICAN REVOLUTION 1910–20

From 1876 to 1911 Mexico was ruled by Porfirio Díaz. The so-called *Porfiriato* saw the country's economy and social structures modernised under a carefully crafted political system in which Díaz – with the exception of four years – repeatedly succeeded in getting himself elected as President. Though an era of relative stability for the country, the conditions for most ordinary people remained poor and unchanged. In 1910 Díaz was challenged by Francisco I Madero. Díaz engineered another victory, but Madero refused to accept this and his defiance helped spark an uprising. In May 1911 the long-time ruler of Mexico finally left the country.

However, the revolution did not herald a period of calm and transparent democracy as the aristocratic Madero had hoped, but instead ushered in a decade of violence, bloodshed and political turmoil. Men such as peasant leader Emiliano Zapata and the flamboyant Francisco 'Pancho' Villa in the north became popular figures in the country with their own following. In 1913 Madero was murdered and his chief of staff, General Victoriano Huerta, seized power with the help of the US Ambassador Henry Lane Wilson (no relation to US President Woodrow Wilson). Amid growing turmoil, Huerta was forced to leave office and was replaced by Venustiano Carranza. Opposed by Villa and Zapata, he would stay in power until 1920.

Carranza's Presidency saw the introduction of the 1917 Constitution, a radical document that allowed for land redistribution, gave new rights to workers, limited land ownership by foreigners and nationalised oil reserves. The instability and chaos of much of these years – as well as the attack on foreign property rights – alarmed Washington. President Wilson's administration intervened twice in Mexico, dispatching troops to Vera Cruz in 1914 to stop a German ship carrying arms, then sending General John J Pershing to attack Villa in 1916 after the latter had launched a raid on American soil. Tensions between Wilson and Carranza were strained, not helped by a feeling in Washington that Mexico, which was to remain resolutely neutral in the First World War, was sympathetic to Germany. Mexico was not invited to join the League of Nations in 1919. By far the biggest Latin country in Central and North America, Mexico's strained relations with the United States inevitably had a complicating effect on regional politics.

An even more dramatic example of intervention was to follow in Nicaragua. The Liberal dictator José Zelaya had long been a thorn in the side of Washington's foreign policy in the region. The United States looked upon him not only as someone who was broadly hostile to American commerce, but also as a destabilising force in the area. Zelaya was suspected of wanting to unite Central America by force, first by combining with Honduras against El Salvador and then ultimately being in a position to take on the more powerful Guatemala. There was little doubt that Zelaya, who genuinely did want a united isthmus, was behind many of the seemingly endless skirmishes, intrigues and armed conflicts that took place in the region in this period. Diplomats in Washington also blamed the dictator for scuppering attempts to produce peacekeeping structures in Central America in which (pre-revolutionary) Mexico and the United States would be arbiters; Zelaya refused to recognise the right of Washington to become involved in regional issues. With construction of the Panama Canal now busily underway, the United States could not tolerate any instability that might threaten its security.

Zelaya was certainly a brutal dictator, who combined some progressive policies – improving education and communications in the country, for example – with more old-fashioned ruthlessness towards opponents, Nicaraguan or otherwise, and corruption. In truth he was probably no better and no worse a ruler than many before and after him in the region. But as far as the United States was concerned, his dislike of foreign commerce and his open hostility to foreign business interests – especially American – marked him out as public enemy number one in Nicaragua. In particular the United States Secretary of State Philander C Knox developed something of an obsession with the Nicaraguan leader. This hostility towards Zelaya dragged the United States into intervention in Nicaragua that would last well beyond the First World War.

In 1909 a Conservative revolt against Zelaya was underway when two American mercenaries were captured by the authorities. The two men were promptly executed by firing squad. Washington was horrified, even more so as a French soldier of fortune captured at the same time was spared the ultimate penalty. To the United States this seemed like a deliberate insult, and the country broke off relations with Nicaragua. President William Howard Taft described Zelaya as a 'medieval despot' while Knox referred to him as a 'blot upon the history of Nicaragua'.[4] Realising that his country probably faced direct military intervention, Zelaya chose to flee and headed for Mexico and exile, ending sixteen years of uncompromising rule.

The end of Zelaya did not mean the end of the conflict, however. Knox, convinced that the 'evil spirit' of the dictator also extended to all his political allies, refused to accept the new Liberal ruler José Madriz, and the Conservative rebellion continued with US marines on standby in the Caribbean port of Bluefields to protect American interests.[5] Eventually, in 1910, the Conservative rebels prevailed and Juan Estrada became the new President with American backing. The instability, however, had created a financial crisis that was followed by a rapid change of president. The new man in charge, Adolfo Díaz, found himself facing insurgency both from the ousted Liberals and disgruntled Conservatives led by General Emiliano Chamorro Vargas, the future President and son of the future Peace Conference delegate Salvador Chamorro. Feeling himself running out of options, Díaz appealed to the United States for military aid to protect US interests and also, he said, to extend that protection to all the country's inhabitants. The result was that in 1912 President Taft sent in the marines to restore order; they stayed in Nicaragua until 1933. This form of direct intervention had been foreseen in a poem written by Rubén Darío in 1904, after Washington's acquisition of the Panama Canal Zone. Entitled 'To Roosevelt', it includes the lines: 'You are the United States, you are the future invader, of the guileless America of indigenous blood, that still prays to Jesus Christ and still speaks in Spanish.'[6]

Foreign involvement in Central America and the Caribbean was certainly not limited to military action, however. For one thing, the American government of William Howard Taft preferred if possible to carry out what both it and critics referred to as 'dollar diplomacy' rather than military involvement. Moreover this was also the start of the era of the so-called 'Banana Republic' in Central America. Though foreign interests had a major stake in coffee production in the region, much of the coffee-growing land involved remained in the hands of local owners. In the banana industry, however, foreign companies controlled much of the land. These firms not only owned and ran the plantations. They built and operated railways, owned shipping lines and in some cases effectively administered an economy within an economy in their host nations. Of these

'Dollar diplomacy' was a term coined under the administration of US President William Howard Taft (1909–13) to describe an emphasis on economic rather than military intervention in its dealings with countries in Central America and the Caribbean. The theory was that if Washington could help pay off those nations' debts to European countries through private American loans and by the United States controlling their customs' duties – usually their main source of income – then it would promote stability in the region. It was a sort of Roosevelt Corollary lite. However critics simply saw it as a way of boosting the power of American finance and business in those countries.

companies the most dominant and influential was the United Fruit Company, or UFCO.

The United Fruit Company (known as Chiquita today) was created in 1899 with the merger of two existing firms, Tropical Trading and Transport and Boston Fruit. UFCO went on to become a huge corporation, later establishing a near monopoly on banana production in the region. Its peak would come after the First World War, but even before then it wielded enormous power. As well as owning railways and ships, it built ports and even, in 1913, set up its own telegraph and radio company. It was able to exert considerable influence on politicians in the countries where it operated, for whom it provided a valued source of state revenue. Overall, the presence of UFCO and other banana firms in Central America served the purposes of most of the Liberal dictators at the time. They brought in income, helped finance economic development, allowed those countries to develop their underdeveloped tropical lowlands and provided infrastructure. But the costs were huge also: a loss of economic and political sovereignty, political meddling and over-dependence on just one industry. Nor was the building of railways, for example, always helpful for anyone other than those who worked in the banana industry, as these railroads tended to go from the plantations to the ports. Cities such as the Honduran capital Tegucigalpa, which was not on the banana trail, had no rail link built. Indeed it was Honduras that became the classic 'Banana Republic'.

Though bananas were grown throughout the region, they were most important to the economies of Panama, Costa Rica and above all Honduras. This country became the major producer in Central America and was the region's only state in which the fruit became the biggest export commodity. A good example of how bananas, money and political power combined in Honduras came in 1911 when President Miguel Dávila (another protégé of the former President Zelaya in Nicaragua) was in office. At this time, an ambitious United States citizen Sam Zemurray was already working in the banana business in the country and was involved in building a railroad of his own. Aware that under Dávila his business fortunes might not prosper – in contrast to some of his rivals – Zemurray cast around for a solution. He found it in the form of an old friend former President Manuel Bonilla and an American soldier of fortune, 'General' Lee Christmas.

Manuel Bonilla was then in exile, living part of the time in British Honduras, though he was already plotting a possible comeback. It seems fairly clear that Zemurray agreed to bankroll Bonilla in his efforts, aided by his friend Christmas, in return for lucrative concessions once the Honduran was restored to power. After an abortive early attempt, Christmas and his band of mercenaries succeeded in staging a revolt that eventually persuaded Dávila to step down as President. Manuel Bonilla was then elected President for the second time. The importance of Zemurray's backing to the Bonilla cause can be seen in the rewards showered upon the American and his new Cuyamel Fruit Company after 1911. He was awarded 10,000 hectares of land to plant bananas along the north coast and was given other concessions too. Bonilla also appointed Zemurray the official agent charged with raising the $500,000 loan to pay the expenses of the recent revolution – including the American's own financial investment in it. It was a win-win situation for Zemurray, who was thus able to get his stake money back, as well as his 'winnings' in gambling on the Bonilla plot.

Manuel Bonilla had long been a bitter rival of his namesake

and future Peace Conference delegate Policarpo Bonilla. The former's use of the American mercenary Lee Christmas had served only to sour the relationship still further. The depth of enmity between Christmas and Policarpo Bonilla had surfaced a few years before, during Manuel Bonilla's first term of office. In February 1904 the President, faced with more unrest and dissent in the country, ordered the closure of the country's National Assembly and the arrest nine of its members. One of these was Policarpo Bonilla – he had been elected to the Assembly the previous year – and the pretext was an alleged plot to kill the President.

The man chosen to lead the soldiers to carry out the arrest was Lee Christmas, who at the time was Manuel Bonilla's chief of police in the capital. Christmas already knew Policarpo Bonilla and had been on the receiving end of the Honduran's recent criticism. As the police chief strode ahead of his men into the legislative chamber, Policarpo immediately spotted him. Instinctively, Christmas raised his Winchester rifle, at which the Honduran

> **You're a dishonour to your race and a miserable dog.**
> POLICARPO BONILLA TO AMERICAN LEE CHRISTMAS

took out his revolver from his coat pocket and mocked the American. *Christmas, you're a dishonour to your race and a miserable dog.* Christmas, who had cultivated the image of a hard man, appeared to be about to shoot Policarpo Bonilla when someone standing next to the American raised his arm, deflecting the weapon away from the politician.[7]

Nonetheless, Christmas was able to get his revenge on Policarpo soon afterwards. As head of the police in Tegucigalpa, Christmas had the right to sit as one of the judges in the alleged conspirators' trial and took some pleasure in handing down a jail sentence on the former President.

President Manuel Bonilla took pity on many of those found guilty, and they were quickly released from detention. Policarpo Bonilla was not so lucky. His estates were seized, he was kept in prison, he was often refused communication with the outside world, and deprived of books or paper to write on. He was not even allowed to bathe or comb his hair for some months. Moreover, contrary to current practice at the time, he was forbidden a conjugal visit from his wife, Emma Gutiérrez Lozano – whom he had married on 27 September 1900 – for several months. Policarpo Bonilla stayed incarcerated like this for two years before eventually being freed and making his way to neighbouring El Salvador.[8]

Policarpo Bonilla was apparently released because, though an ally of the powerful President Zelaya of Nicaragua, it was felt that his power had been 'forever broken'. It was certainly true that unlike his namesake Manuel Bonilla, Policarpo would never again become President of his country. But his enemies were wrong in assuming he was a beaten man. In fact, Policarpo was to continue plotting his return as President for some years to come and was still to play a prominent role in Honduran life, albeit often from abroad. Indeed, when President Dávila took over the Presidency of Honduras in 1907, some assumed that he was just temporarily holding office until his ally President Zelaya in Nicaragua could arrange for his old friend and protégé Policarpo Bonilla to take over. Ultimately Dávila stayed in power but Policarpo, who was living in Tegucigalpa at the time, did not give up hope of regaining the top job.[9] Indeed, back in 1910 Honduras's beleaguered President found himself in the bizarre situation of facing potential rebellion from two former Presidents, both of whom were called Bonilla. In the end, of course, it was the efforts of Manuel Bonilla, Christmas and Zemurray that proved successful. But Policarpo had also been scheming behind the scenes for a possible takeover. Then, in June 1911, he was reported to be at a house in New Orleans, plotting his next move.

This southern American city had long enjoyed strong links with Honduras and other parts of Central America. The opening up of the Caribbean coast of Honduras to the banana trade and the use of regular shipping lanes for trade meant that New Orleans was more accessible to some Hondurans than other parts of their own country and certainly many other parts of Central America. In time, New Orleans became a key place for the banana trade but also the location of choice for many disgruntled Central American politicians to plot rebellion and revolution; in particular, men from Honduras and Nicaragua. 'Revolution is in the air all night long,' wrote one journalist in an article, 'New Orleans – where the revolutions come from.' He continued, 'Well-known groups of generals may be seen in the café corners looking wise and secret, and drinking silent toasts to something or other.' The reporter, referring to the recent revolt in Honduras by Manuel Bonilla and Lee Christmas, said that afterwards things had quietened down, '... until Gen Policarpo Bonilla ... ex-President of Honduras and ex-friend of Manuel Bonilla, who is now in high feather, struck town a few days ago. Then things got busy ...'.[10]

The reporter suspected that Policarpo was plotting to overthrow the new ruler in Nicaragua, as part of a bigger plan for him and his Liberal allies, such as Zelaya, to take control of Guatemala, Honduras and El Salvador. Cited as evidence was the fact that Policarpo was staying with a former consular representative of Nicaragua in a house in the city's Canal Street owned by former President Zelaya. 'Gen. Policarpo

Bonilla is reported to be an avowed agent of Zelaya and, it is believed, wants to even up old scores with the men who made it possible for Gen. Manuel Bonilla to regain power in Honduras and who drove Zelaya's crowd out of that country.' The reporter added, 'Policarpo Bonilla does not confine his activities to New Orleans, though his headquarters are there. He has been making trips to Chicago, Mobile and El Paso.'[11] Ultimately little came of this latest plotting. But after his bitter rival Manuel Bonilla died in office in 1913, Policarpo Bonilla's fortunes under the next ruler Francisco Bertrand Barahona were to revive.

The frequent changes of government in Honduras stood in contrast to events in Guatemala, where the ruthless dictator Manuel Estrada Cabrera had been in power since 1898 and where he would remain in charge until 1920. Estrada Cabrera was broadly sympathetic to business interests and under his rule American companies such as UFCO flourished. However, though he ruled for twenty-two years, the dictator faced challenges to his authority, notably in 1906, when he thwarted a rebellion launched from neighbouring countries, part of the seemingly never-ending disputes and quarrels that beset Central America at this time. Among the more curious aspects of his long dictatorship were Estrada Cabrera's attempts to encourage a cult devoted to Minerva. The dictator saw the education of his people as one of his key missions, hence his quixotic decision to turn to the Roman goddess of wisdom for inspiration.

Future Paris delegate Joaquín Méndez had been a minister of public works under the ruthless Estrada Cabrera, but by 1911 he had moved to Washington to take up the post of Guatemalan Minister to the United States. Given the importance of United States-Guatemala relations, it was a key post and indicates that Méndez was both highly regarded and trusted by the regime. He proved himself to be a shrewd and capable diplomat who knew how to follow instructions from his masters. In February 1912, for example, Méndez was fully supportive of a planned tour by US Secretary of State Knox of nations bordering the Caribbean. *I believe the visit will be fruitful of results in those countries which within a short time will receive a great stimulus through the opening of the Panama Canal*, he told journalists.[12] His own personal ties with the United States increased when he married an American woman, Elizabeth Kramer.

In stark contrast with the enduring if stifling stability of Guatemala under the rule of Estrada Cabrera, Haiti was falling further and further into chaos. The problems seemed growing and insurmountable: massive overseas debt leading to interference from foreign powers, incessant political tensions and a culture of political violence which meant it was increasingly difficult to maintain any political stability. The stark figures tell part of the story: between 1902 and the beginning of 1915 the state had eight different presidents, none of whom served full terms. A report in *The Times* of 1908 reveals the extent of hostility that the country's rulers could excite among the people. It describes how deposed President Pierre Nord Alexis was taken to the safety of a French ship by the French Minister in Haiti, who threw a French Tricolour over his shoulder to help protect the fleeing ruler as they reached the harbour. 'The people tried to hurl themselves upon him, fighting with hands and feet the soldiers ... President Alexis, still draped in the Tricolour, boarded a skiff, his suite tumbling in after him. Haitian, French and American warships fired a salute to the fallen president. As he was embarking a woman aimed a blow at his side with a knife but missed him.

A man however succeeded in striking the president a glancing blow on his neck with his fist.' [13] Meanwhile a few years later, in 1912, Cincinnatus Leconte, perhaps the most promising President Haiti had elected in some time, died in a freak explosion at the National Palace.

A key problem for Haiti was undoubtedly the meddling of foreign powers concerned about both their business interests there and the amount of money that Haiti owed them. Britain, France, Germany, Italy and the United States all took a close interest in the state. For Germany, a European power arriving late in the scramble for empire, Haiti also offered an opportunity to exert real influence in a country that was not yet under the direct sphere of influence of any one nation. Though the German community in Haiti was small – perhaps no more than 200 in 1910 – it exerted considerable influence. Germans controlled about 80 percent of the country's international commerce and owned and operated utilities.

Within a few years, the deteriorating situation in Haiti would lead the United States to pursue the doctrine of the Roosevelt Corollary and intervene militarily, partly because of fears that if they did not, other powers would. By then, in any case, the international scene had changed dramatically and permanently with the start of a major war in Europe. Though far from the fighting, the Central American and Caribbean powers would find that their proximity to the United States would eventually lead to them being pulled into the conflict.

3

Follow My Leader 1914–1918

From the outbreak of the conflict in August 1914, the First World War attracted the close attention of politicians and many others in Central America and the Caribbean. One reason was the dependence that many countries in the region had on the major European countries in terms of trade. Much of the coffee produced in Central America, for example, found its way to the coffee houses and breakfast rooms of Britain, Germany and France. Any disruption to world trade caused by the conflict would certainly impact on the region's prosperity. Another factor was the presence of a considerable number of European diplomats, business people, professionals and private citizens across the region, whose relationship with each other and with their host countries would be affected by the war.

An additional reason why many in the region were interested in the faraway conflict was a shared cultural and political history; many of the elites in Central America and the Caribbean looked upon Europe as their place of origin, the home of many of the ideas and philosophies to which they adhered. Finally, the opening of the Panama Canal as the conduit between the Atlantic and Pacific Oceans on 15 August 1914, by a curious coincidence just days before the outbreak of war, hugely increased the area's strategic importance.

Yet despite the keen attention given to the war by the region's ruling elites and business communities, the prospect of being drawn directly into a conflict on the other side of the Atlantic Ocean seemed remote. The main reason for this, inevitably, was the status of the United States. Once Washington made it clear in 1914 that the US would stay neutral in the European war, it was all but certain that Central American countries would adopt a similar stance. Cuba and Nicaragua, of course, were already under the protection of Washington so their position was practically guaranteed; but in fact all six countries under discussion made it clear they would stay resolutely neutral. As Percy Martin, a leading historian of the impact of the First World war on the region, observed, '… any other attitude would have been unthinkable so long as the United States held aloof from the struggle.' [1] This did not mean, of course, that the neutral Americas could escape all aspects of the war. Apart from the obvious and crucial impact on trade – the start of the war would provoke a world financial crisis – the presence of German, British and French interests in the region ensured there would be some fallout from the war, even at this distance from the trenches of Western

LATIN AMERICA AND THE WAR
In South America the only nation to declare war on Germany during the First World War was Portuguese-speaking Brazil. Four other countries broke off relations with Germany: Bolivia, Ecuador, Peru and Uruguay. The most powerful Spanish-speaking South American country, Argentina, stayed neutral, as did its neighbour Chile; Colombia, whose resentment toward the United States stemmed from the independence of Panama; Venezuela; and Paraguay. In Central America El Salvador remained neutral, while Costa Rica declared war on Germany. Further to the north, Mexico was also officially neutral.

Europe. To a limited extent the European powers would take part in a proxy war in Latin America.

There was also the, albeit limited, factor of public opinion to take into account. Among those who took an interest in events in Europe, the majority sided with the Allies and especially France. For all its imperial meddling and economic demands subsequently, France was still the land of liberty and independence for most Central Americans – the Enlightenment and the French Revolution had played a psychological and philosophical role in the Spanish American wars of independence. Probably the only real exception to the broadly pro-French stance was in Guatemala, where there was at the start of the war considerable sympathy for Germany, though even there it was probably not the majority sentiment.

In Haiti there was considerable suspicion about likely German actions against the state. As we have seen, Germany had maintained a powerful presence in the nation for a number of years. Aside from its business interests, there were suggestions that Berlin had helped bankroll the overthrow of two administrations, in 1908 and 1912. There were now, at the beginning of the war, rumours that Germany was looking for an excuse to establish Haiti as a protectorate and build a coaling station there to refuel its ships in the region. Mistrust of German motives was also held by the other foreign powers on the island. When in 1914 around 200 Haitians walked into the French Legation in Port-au-Prince volunteering for service in Europe, they were rejected on the grounds that the President, Oreste Zamor, had accepted money from Berlin to help pay the country's debt.[2] Nonetheless, a number of Haitians did serve as volunteers in the French army in Europe.

Indeed, it was concern over potential direct German action in Haiti that was in part behind the most important event that occurred there during the First World War – the intervention of United States marines in 1915. By that date Washington had become increasingly worried that Germany would exploit the rapidly deteriorating security situation in Haiti. Years later former US Secretary of State Robert Lansing made this clear when he gave written evidence to a Senate Committee. Lansing said, '... I refer to the attitude of the Imperial German Government in connection with the political disorders and financial straits of Haiti and the pretexts for aggression thereby afforded. There was good reason to believe that in the years 1913–1914 Germany was ready to go to great lengths to secure the exclusive customs control of Haiti and also to secure coaling stations at Mole St Nicholas.' One of the two reasons, Lansing said, that the US had felt obliged to intervene was a 'desire to forestall any attempt by a foreign power to obtain a foothold on the territory of an American nation ...'[3]

The other ostensible reason for the landing of US marines in July 1915 was the appalling state of security on the island. The country's pro-American President Jean Vilbrun Guillaume Sam had taken office in February 1915 amid chronic instability. Facing opposition to his rule, Sam reacted with harsh brutality, culminating in the execution of 167 political prisoners, many of them from prominent families, a slaughter carried out on the orders of one of the army commanders. Sam fled to the apparent safety of the French Legation but an angry crowd, incensed by the killings, tore into the building and dragged the President from his hiding place. The hapless man was then literally torn to pieces in the street and his body parts paraded around Port-au-Prince. Back in Washington, President Woodrow Wilson had had enough. The following day, 28 July 1915, American warships landed marines on Haitian soil, where they were to remain for nearly two decades. To the cynical this was simply an opportunistic act, taking advantage of unrest and a perceived threat from foreign powers to protect American commercial interests close to home. Washington, however, justified it as an attempt to restore law and order in a neighbouring state, as well as a move to prevent Germany from seizing control of a strategically vital country.

The arrival of the marines and the election of pro-American President Philippe Sudre Dartiguenave suggested that Haiti would closely follow the policy of the United States in the war. This seemed even more likely after the sinking of the French steamship *SS Karnak* by a German submarine off Malta in November 1916 and the loss of the steamship *SS Montreal* together cost the lives of eight Haitians and valuable Haitian cargo. Yet when the United States declared war on Germany in April 1917 and President Sudre Dartiguenave asked the Haitian National Assembly to follow suit it refused, limiting itself to a protest against the German submarine campaign. This did not, though, stop the President instructing the Haitian Chargé d'Affaires in Berlin Monsieur Fouchard to ask for compensation for the Haitian loss of life and property and for guarantees that Germany would abide by international conventions. The diplomat was simply handed his papers. It was not until 13 July 1918 that Haiti finally declared war on Germany, well over a year after its protector the United States had done so. By then the uncooperative National Assembly had been dissolved to be replaced by a Council of State, whose members were hand-picked by the President. Evidently, even though it was under the effective control of Washington, there were still strong voices of dissent within Haiti.

Nonetheless, there were a number of anti-German measures carried out there. Eight German businesses on the island were sequestrated and a number of prominent German businessmen interned. American troops were also on the alert after persistent rumours that Germany was trying to create a submarine base on Haiti and planned an invasion. No real evidence of any plots was unearthed, though two Germans were sentenced for trying to leave the country in a small boat, allegedly with incriminating maps in their possession. In another curious incident, it was discovered that a number of Germans had sung their national anthem at a Christmas Eve party hosted by one of them. The homeowner was threatened with court action if there was any repetition of the episode. Some Americans, meanwhile, hoped that the war and their occupation had provided an opportunity to remove German influence on Haiti permanently.[4]

The years immediately leading up to and the beginning of the First World War were a busy time for one of Haiti's most prominent citizens, Tertulien Guilbaud. The former Senator had been named Education Minister and Justice Minister in 1911, positions he held for two years during a succession of Haiti's revolving-door presidencies. Twice in this period, too, he was, as a senior Minister, a member of the Council of Secretaries of States that briefly ran the country in between presidencies. During his time as Education Minister, Guilbaud carried out a number of significant reforms, including the creation of a teacher training college that eventually opened in 1914 after he left office. As Justice Minister he also set up a commission to overhaul the country's criminal law code. Later, in March 1915, he briefly joined the ill-fated administration of Jean Vilbrun Guillaume Sam as Education Minister again, but swiftly fell out with the President and left two months later. However Guilbaud had made good contacts with the diplomatic corps in Port-au-Prince, which, combined with his years of exemplary service and high standing in Haiti, led to him being offered the presidency of the country soon after the American invasion. Guilbaud, however, immediately turned down the offer, describing the position as one of *an excess of honour and indignity*. Guilbaud was a patriot and according to the Haitian *Dictionary of Biography* he refused to 'collaborate' with the forces of the United States and become their 'vassal president'.[5] However, Guilbaud did later accept an offer to become his country's Minister to France, meaning a return to Paris, a city which he knew well from his days as a law student.

> **'Tertulien Guilbaud refused to collaborate with the Americans and become their vassal.'**
>
> DICTIONARY OF BIOGRAPHY, NATIONAL LIBRARY OF HAITI

Fears that Germany would use the region as a means of attacking American interests during the war were not just confined to Haiti. Probably the biggest perceived threat was seen in Guatemala, where public sympathy for the Central Powers was perhaps the strongest in the region. At the outbreak of the war the country's dictator Manuel Estrada Cabrera certainly kept a strictly neutral line. The ruthless but shrewd dictator clearly saw no need to take sides in a dispute when his country traded with both sides of the conflict, as well as the neutral United States. In fact, if anything the country appeared to favour the Germans, with propaganda from the German side allowed to circulate fairly freely in the country. There is also reason to believe that Estrada Cabrera probably had personal sympathies with the military ethos of Germany.[6] However, he was too wily to risk publicly upsetting the Allies and the United States, and in 1915 he discreetly declined to renew a trade agreement with Berlin that gave German businessmen favourable terms in the country. The mood in Guatemala and across Central and North America then changed significantly early in 1917 with the publication of what became known as the Zimmermann Telegram.

The United States had already been worried about the potential for Mexico to create mischief in the region and even in its own territory after that country's revolution, and this had been reinforced now there was a major world conflict. Yet Woodrow Wilson had been re-elected in 1916 partly because he had kept the United States out of the war, and there seemed no imminent prospect of Washington wanting to join the conflict. In early 1917, however, the German decision to resume unrestricted submarine warfare against shipping placed all nations' vessels at risk and helped turn the tide of public opinion in the United States and other countries against Berlin. Aware that the United States might ultimately join the Allied side, the German authorities hatched a plan to use Mexico to tie down American troops in the future.

The idea was simple if audacious: Germany secretly offered the Mexican President Venustiano Carranza generous financial support in return for that country taking up arms against the United States to regain lands it had previously lost in New Mexico, Texas and Arizona. This offer was conveyed from the German Foreign Minister Arthur Zimmermann to the German Ambassador in Washington, and then, in January 1917, passed onto the German representative in Mexico in order for it to be put to the Mexican authorities. Unfortunately for the Germans, the telegram was intercepted and deciphered by the British. In February – after the start of the German submarine campaign – the British revealed the contents of the message to Washington, which then leaked these to the press at the beginning of March. Inevitably it provoked a public uproar.[7]

The publication of the telegram played a role in the decision made by the United States the following month to declare war on Germany. It also highlighted the fact that Mexico was – potentially – Washington's Achilles heel in the region. The Mexican position regarding the war was and remained strictly neutral, and there is little evidence that Mexico ever seriously considered adopting any other stance. Yet both the British and Americans feared Mexico would nonetheless allow Germany to use its waters as a base for submarine warfare. Though the threat was undoubtedly exaggerated, there is also no doubt that German spies operated a significant network in Mexico and that German propaganda against the Allies was prevalent.[8]

Once the Zimmermann Telegram was made public, reports of other plots – more or less fanciful – were published in newspapers as international tensions mounted. One directly involved Guatemala. The country had historically had tense relations with Mexico, its far larger and more powerful neighbour to the north. Under a headline that read 'Plotting in Many lands: Central and South America and East Indies Infested by Germans' *The New York Times* reported in March 1917 that Germany had tried to persuade President Carranza of Mexico to invade Guatemala and overthrow the Estrada Cabrera regime, with the promise that if Germany won the war then Mexico could keep the lands that had once been under its control in the days of the Spanish Empire. It was also claimed that Germany, with Mexican help, was trying to persuade El Salvador to adopt a 'hostile attitude' towards Guatemala. The newspaper further stated that Germany wanted to 'use [El Salvador] as a base against both

Guatemala and Nicaragua for the fomenting of trouble calculated to favor Mexico and to embarrass the United States'.[9]

Though it is hard now to know just how real these particular plots were, it appears that President Estrada Cabrera, who
was closely informed of events and the mood in Washington
by his Minister Joaquín Méndez, genuinely feared aggression from El Salvador and Mexico. He was also aware that
a German spy network existed not just in Mexico but in his
own country too. As historian Martin put it, 'Throughout
the early years of the war Guatemala was the centre of an
elaborately developed espionage system, whose ramifications
extended throughout Central America.' The man behind
this network was said to be the German Minister to Central
America, Kurt Lehmann, who also played a prominent role in
promoting German propaganda across the region.[10]

Perhaps sensing that the time was coming when he might
have to choose sides, Estrada Cabrera began positioning Guatemala closer to the United States and the Allies. In March
1917 the dictator's Foreign Minister made a formal protest to
Lehmann about Germany's submarine campaign, a protest
that the diplomat refused even to acknowledge. Then, after
the United States declared war on Germany, Guatemala, too,
severed relations with Berlin. In Washington Joaquín Méndez
was careful to make sure the administration there knew that
Guatemala was simply maintaining a policy it had pursued
from the start of the war. *I take pleasure in reiterating that
Guatemala from the first has adhered to and supported the
attitude of the United States in the defense of the rights of
nations, the liberty of the seas, and of international justice
...* he wrote to Secretary of State Lansing. Méndez added,
*... Guatemala takes the greatest pleasure in offering the
United States her territorial waters, her ports, and railways*

for use in common defense … . Meanwhile in a public statement Méndez said that his country had adopted this stance *on account of the plots of the Germans against the safety and independence not only of Guatemala, but of the whole of Central America* … .[11]

Estrada Cabrera decided to back the United States so clearly for a number of reasons. One was his fear of Mexico and El Salvador, another was the chance

> Guatemala takes the greatest pleasure in offering the United States her territorial waters, her ports, and railways for use in common defense … .
>
> JOAQUÍN MÉNDEZ

to curry favour with the United States and perhaps thus obtain more favourable trade terms, as well as gain protection. But equally important was a third factor: the chance to confiscate large German-owned estates in his country. Like any self-respecting dictator, Estrada Cabrera tolerated, rather than enjoyed, the necessary evil of foreign interference in his country's domestic business. Here was an opportunity to reduce or even remove German influence in his country, and one he soon took. On 23 April 1918 the country formally declared war on Germany.

Though the threat from German spies and propaganda – however exaggerated – caused great concern in the region during the First World War, the Allies themselves were not slow at using similar tactics, both to keep themselves informed of events and to try to win over important sections of society. The British government was actively involved in transmitting propaganda throughout Latin America, including Mexico and Central America. A Foreign Office secret memo in 1916 revealed that 'telegraphic propaganda' was being sent via a 'subsidized Reuters service' to newspapers across South America and that a 'similar service and on a similar scale has lately been started for Central America and Mexico, with distributing centre at Panama'. However while the author of the memo felt that such propaganda in South America was not so necessary as in other parts of the world 'feelings being quite strongly for the Allies ... or at least not hostile', the same could not be said for Central America. Here there was 'still work to be done' in a region where 'the German trade hold is still strong'.[12]

As for the Americans, the years of neutrality at the start of the war had left them dangerously short of information about what was really going on in the region. For example, in January 1917, only three months before Washington entered the war, the Office of Naval Intelligence (ONI) had a small network of military attachés gathering information from just a handful of spies. However within a few months, as war loomed, the ONI had rapidly recruited a network of 85 agents around the world, including spies in Mexico, Central America, Cuba and Haiti, as well as a number of South American countries. Some would later turn out to be 'useless' and others would essentially sit back and take the money on offer. But a number of the agents turned out to be very talented, even if some of the intelligence gleaned turned out to be bizarre on occasions. One report, for example, claimed that German submarines were being secretly shipped to Guatemala, smuggled into Mexico and then put into service there by local engineers under a German supervisor. Given the antipathy between the regimes in Mexico and Guatemala, this stretched credulity. Taken more seriously, however, were reports in September 1917 that Germany planned to establish submarine bases on the coast of Mexico, though no evidence was ever found of them. The Americans even sent a spy to Guatemala who was a radio expert. In Guatemala City he built a large radio station, as well as several smaller ones around the country, with the express aim of monitoring possible German activity and submarine bases.[13]

The nature of the rival propaganda campaigns at the time in the region led a French diplomat to describe it as a 'publicity contest' for the minds of Central Americans. Numerous speakers, pamphlets and newspapers in Guatemala, for example, sought to persuade local people it was best to be on friendly terms with Germany and to remain neutral in the war. Similar attempts to influence public opinion were carried out in Honduras and Nicaragua. On the other side, a group of British, Belgian and French citizens in Guatemala joined together to publish *Le National* newspaper to counter the German propaganda.[14]

For the United States – and the Allies as a whole – arguably the most strategically important country of the six discussed here was Panama. The newly opened canal across the country had to be protected and kept open for US shipping. The Canal Zone itself was already guarded by the US, but it was important, too, that the government in Panama itself was sympathetic to Washington. On this front, the United States had little to fear, as Panamanian foreign policy in this period was difficult to distinguish from that of her big ally to the north. On 23 February 1917, a few weeks after the United States broke off relations with Germany, President Ramón Valdés, who had taken up office just a few months earlier, sent a message to the country's National Assembly that spoke of Panama's 'loyalty' to the United States. The Assembly duly passed a resolution of sympathy for the United States and her people. On 6 April, the day Washington declared war, President Valdés cabled President Woodrow to underline his country's 'determination' to defend against 'any hostile attack which has as its object the Panama Canal.'[15] Curiously, though the next day Panama clearly identified itself with the position of the United States and as a belligerent, it initially made no formal declaration of war at this time. As the President effectively stated that its interests were identical with those of Washington, it perhaps felt no need. On 7 November 1917 the country's National Assembly approved the executive's actions, making it clear that Valdés's proclamation on 7 April had amounted to a declaration of war. On 10 December Panama followed the United States' lead by declaring war on Austria-Hungary.

Though reassured by Panama's swift support, the United States was in no mood to take any chances. So when a number of German nationals were immediately interned by Panama on the island of Taboga, twelve miles off the Panama coast, the American authorities intervened to have them transferred to the United States. It was felt that even on Taboga the interned Germans were too close to the canal. The Panamanian government meanwhile enforced censorship of the mail across the country in August 1917 – it was already in practice in the Canal Zone – and later obliged all remaining German nationals or nationals of Germany's allies to register with their local provincial governor. Though Valdés died before the war was over, the country remained staunchly loyal to Washington throughout the conflict.

Cuba's proximity to the United States mainland also made that island crucial strategically as Washington's involvement in the war became ever more likely in early 1917. However, in February of that year armed conflict broke out in Cuba itself, when the Liberals, frustrated at what they saw as electoral fraud carried out to get the Conservative ruler Mario García Menocal re-elected the previous year, staged a revolt.

The attempt to overthrow the government was soon defeated, with Menocal able to buy 10,000 rifles from Washington and with the United States also landing a small contingent of marines to ensure order.

Though there was no evidence for it, it was claimed in some countries – for example in Britain – that the revolt had been instigated by agents from Berlin. It was a claim not taken seriously in Washington, or even by conservative elements in Cuba. There was, though, concern that German spies forced to flee the United States might seek refuge in Cuba and from there communicate with fellow agents in Mexico who in turn were in direct contact with Berlin. Menocal, aware of how much he needed American backing, thus chose to make sure Washington had little cause to doubt him when it came to support in the First World War. Within a day of Washington declaring war on Germany on 6 April, both houses of the country's legislature, at Menocal's request, had also passed a resolution declaring war.

Cuba later imposed tough restrictions on German citizens on the island, notably the Espionage Act of July 1918 which forbad enemy aliens from, among other things, living within half a mile of any fortress, munitions store, shipyard or even factory. Provisions were also made to take care of those possessions belonging to enemy aliens who were interned during the war. The person put in charge of these possessions was the future delegate to Paris, Dr Antonio Sánchez de Bustamante y Sirvén. By this time Bustamante had already earned a formidable reputation as a lawyer – he was the dean of the law faculty at the University of Havana, one of the universities where he had originally studied law. Bustamante's role as *inventor de la propriedad enemiga* in 1918 also involved him overseeing all correspondence to or from the prisoners or internees when they contained money or financial securities. Though the position was unpaid, it carried with it considerable moral authority. Bustamante's appointment to the post is an indication of the esteem in which he was held and also his reputation for honesty.

On the other side of the Caribbean, Honduras had been enjoying a less eventful wartime than Cuba. After the death in office in 1913 of Policarpo Bonilla's old enemy President Manuel Bonilla, the new man at the helm was Francisco Bertrand Barahona. He had been Manuel Bonilla's Vice-President and was elected in his own right in late 1915. Bertrand and his Foreign Minister, Mariano Vásquez, steered a cautious line during the First World War, always anxious to keep on the right side of the United States but not showing the kind of enthusiasm for following the Washington line seen in Cuba or Panama. When the Americans broke relations with Germany in early 1917, Vásquez made clear that his country 'approved' of the move. But it was not until 17 May – more than a month after the United States entered the war – that Honduras severed diplomatic relations with Berlin.

The delay before Honduras finally declared war on Germany was even longer. It was only on 19 July 1918 that the authorities in Tegucigalpa made the official declaration. Exactly why the Honduran government took so long to follow the United States is unclear, though it suggests a certain lack of enthusiasm for getting too closely involved in the war. There had been strands of anti-Americanism or at least coolness towards the United States in Honduran public life in the past, particularly shown by former President Policarpo Bonilla. However there is no evidence that Bonilla, whose political star had been on the ascendant since the death of his namesake in 1913, had any say in a decision by a government of which he was not a part. Equally, what prompted Honduras to enter the war when it did, given that it had delayed so long, is not clear. The official reason was to show solidarity with the United States. Another reason may simply have been the desire to be part of the winning side, and thus take advantage of any benefits that might arise – for example, being invited to a subsequent peace congress.

Perhaps the most likely reason was that it gave the Honduran authorities greater freedom in dealing with German-owned businesses and lands in the country. Though Honduras had not experienced the economic penetration by Germans seen in Guatemala, nevertheless there was a considerable presence there. Many of the German businesses were centred around the island port of Amapala on the Pacific coast. There is some evidence that Honduras used the declaration of war to cause the maximum disruption to these businesses. One other facet of Honduran involvement in the war came to light in August 1918 when President Bertrand authorised the export to the United States of nuts from a certain type of palm tree apparently used to make poison gas.[16]

If Policarpo Bonilla had not been directly involved with Honduran politics, he had been concerned with the politics of a neighbouring country, Nicaragua. Since the occupation of the country by United States marines before the war, it had of course been a staunch ally of Washington. The US State Department wanted to cement this relationship with a treaty. The aim of this treaty was to give Washington the exclusive right to build a canal across the country, plus establish a naval base on the island of Fonseca. In return the Nicaraguans would receive three million dollars to help pay its foreign debt. Washington did not want to build another canal – it controlled the one in Panama – but wanted to ensure that no other country could build a competing one in the only other country most suited geographically for such a construction.

The proposed treaty caused considerable outrage in Central America, particularly in El Salvador, which was especially opposed to the naval base, and Costa Rica, which among other issues was angry it had not been consulted. Of general concern was a provision that would give Washington virtually the same right to intervene in Nicaragua as the notorious Platt Amendment provided in Cuba. One of the biggest opponents to the treaty was Policarpo Bonilla. For many years he had worked towards creating a united region-wide republic. For him, this treaty between Nicaragua and the United States was a major blow. According to one report he feared that the deal would *separate Nicaragua from the other Central American countries and defeat plans for a union of Central American Republics*. Bonilla's stature and track record on this issue persuaded other leaders in the region to allow him to be their main representative fighting the proposal. On 15 January 1914 Bonilla was staying at the Hotel Pierrepont in New York lobbying against the treaty when he received a cable informing him he had been named the representative in the United States for the Patriotic League of Central America 'to defend the interests of Central America'.[17]

In fact the League, Bonilla and neighbouring countries were not the only ones to oppose the treaty. The US Senate also objected to the Platt Amendment-style provisions, and when the deal was signed in August 1914 that aspect of the treaty had been dropped. Finally ratified in 1916, the agreement was known as the Bryan-Chamorro Treaty after US Secretary of State William Jennings Bryan and the Nicaraguan Minister to Washington who signed it, Emiliano Chamorro. Chamorro had originally been opposed to the regime in

Nicaragua – under President Díaz – but had changed his mind. His reward had been the posting to Washington where he was a key figure in the treaty negotiations. Emiliano Chamorro later returned home to become President in January 1917, meaning he was in power when the country broke off relations with Germany in May of that year. Given the country's status and the treaty Chamorro had signed, it was virtually unthinkable for it to follow any other course of action. Then, on 8 March 1918, Nicaragua took the final step and declared war on both Germany and Austria-Hungary, with President Chamorro announcing a state of siege.

One other country in the region declared war on Germany two months after Nicaragua. That was Costa Rica. It was a curious declaration of war because though it was recognised by the country at whom it was aimed – Germany – it was not recognised by a supposed ally, the United States. The reason was that Washington had not recognised the government in Costa Rica where the Minister of War Federico Tinoco Granados had seized power on 27 January 1917. Germany, however, had. Federico Tinoco and his brother Joaquín quickly realised that they needed the approval of Washington if their regime were to survive. So on 21 September 1917 Costa Rica severed relations with Germany and then the following spring, on 23 May, it declared war. The Tinoco regime also closed a number of radio stations it claimed were suspicious and kept a number of German citizens under close watch. All was carried out with the intention of winning favour in Washington and gaining recognition for the government. However, the Wilson Administration remained unmoved, and its refusal to recognise the Tinoco government was to have a major impact on Costa Rica's treatment at the end of the war.

As the war in Europe came to its climax in 1918, the end of the conflict was not the only matter preoccupying the minds of politicians in the region. The growing influence of the United States in the Caribbean and the isthmus, the seemingly endless conflicts and squabbles between Central American Republics and the fragile state of society in Haiti were all pressing matters closer to home. El Salvador, for example, which remained neutral in the war, was deeply dismayed by the refusal of the United States to accept a verdict by the relatively new Central American Court of Justice that the Bryan-Chamorro Treaty had violated El Salvador's rights.

The Central American Court of Justice, set up in 1907, was an ambitious regional attempt to establish a way of restoring or maintaining peace among the often quarrelling five Central American states of Costa Rica, El Salvador, Guatemala, Honduras and Nicaragua. Based in Costa Rica, it was credited with keeping the republics from coming to war for some years. However when it ruled in favour of Costa Rica, El Salvador and Honduras against the US-Nicaraguan Bryan-Chamorro Treaty in 1916, Washington simply ignored the ruling and Managua withdrew from the Court, bringing about its demise.

In Guatemala, meanwhile, the country was still coming to terms with the huge earthquakes that caused extensive damage to Guatemala City in December 1917 and January 1918. El Salvador, too, had been hit by a major earthquake in June 1917. Yet as the guns fell silent in Europe, the diplomatic corridors of the region were beginning to fill with speculation about what the 'rewards' would be for these countries who had declared war and ended up on the victorious side. There was talk of a conference in Europe to settle matters between the Great Powers. But just who would be invited?

Senor Don Emiliano Chamorro.

II
The Paris Peace Conference

4

Getting Heard

Once the war was over, the Allies had to decide how to handle the peace. That there should be some form of conference or congress to discuss the terms of the peace, how the defeated enemies should be treated and to discuss what, if any, new international structures might be put in place to resolve world disputes in future was not in any real doubt. It was even decided fairly early on, in early November, that the gathering should take place in Paris, despite objections from the British. Far less clear would be the size of the conference, the date when it should start – and, above all, who exactly should be invited to it.

The identity of the major participants such as France, Britain and the United States was clear enough. But what about countries such as Uruguay which had broken off relations with Germany but not declared war? Or even those small countries that had declared war, but which realistically had contributed nothing to the war effort and for whom the horrors of trench warfare – still so vivid in the minds of a horror-struck European populace – were so remote? The six countries under discussion here – Guatemala, Honduras,

Nicaragua, Panama, Cuba and Haiti – were all in this last position, with their decision to go to war more a reflection of their relationship with Washington than an attempt to join the fighting itself. Apart from some measures taken against German nationals on their territory, described in the previous chapter, none of the countries had played any military role in the war. None of them could expect to play a major role in forthcoming gathering – whenever it was. For them the big prize would simply be a seat at the table of a gathering of the world's most powerful nations. In other words, the key issue was getting invited.

As in their region, so with invitations to the Peace Conference: the critical viewpoint was that of the United States. Only with the backing of Washington could these six countries hope to be at such a meeting, given the near-total indifference of France and Britain to their participation. At the start, the United States sought to make a distinction between those Latin American countries that had simply broken off relations with Germany – such as Uruguay and Peru – and those which had gone to war, such as Brazil and the six Central American and Caribbean nations under discussion.

Thus at the end of November, when the precise timing and scope of the conference was still unclear, US Secretary of State Lansing sent out two different messages for his Latin American Ambassadors to convey to their hosts. For countries such as Uruguay – which was already anxiously lobbying to be invited – that had broken off relations with Germany the message was simple; there had simply been no discussion yet as to whether such countries should be invited to the conference. Thus it was impossible to say what their prospects were. However, the American diplomats in the Central American and Caribbean nations that declared war were given a slightly more positive message to convey. True, the diplomats were told to tell the relevant countries that it was felt unlikely that the 'preliminary conferences' planned would require their presence. However the note went on to add more hopefully, 'Should it be found necessary to require the presence of representatives from all the belligerent governments, the United States will take great pleasure in transmitting such information to its representatives in all those countries which have declared war against Germany.' Whether the six nations' Foreign Ministries would have been reassured had they seen a memo from Woodrow Wilson's Special Representative Colonel Edward House to Robert Lansing a couple of weeks earlier is doubtful. Though his note stated that a place 'must be ... reserved' for all those who declared war against Germany, even what it called the 'theoretical belligerents' such as China, Brazil and Liberia, it was dismissive about their degree of representation. 'Cuba, Panama, Guatemala, Nicaragua, Costa Rica, Haiti, Honduras ... might be represented by the United States to avoid crowding,' it noted in passing. It was the clearest possible evidence both of how the United States viewed the region and of how little was expected from these smaller nations in Paris. Adding insult to injury, House's note described all these countries as 'South American' even though they are in fact all either Central American or Caribbean states.[1]

Despite the personal suggestion in House's note that the United States could represent the Central American and Caribbean countries, the State Department and other parts of the US government were generally keen for the Latin American countries to be present at the conference. Treaty lawyer and adviser to the American Commission David Hunter Miller considered it to be of 'great importance' to the United States

that the 'Latin American powers should receive the consideration which they expect'. However he was also aware of the
political realities and in particular how other countries saw
Washington's relations with some of the smaller nations. 'It
is, of course, true that … Cuba, Haiti and Panama are practically under the direction of the United States, and this might
also be said of Nicaragua, but this fact is hardly one which
can by us be emphasized according to the suggestions of the
French Note …,' he wrote.[2]

By late December the position of the Americans had
indeed moved decisively towards allowing the six Central
American and Caribbean states to be invited. A briefing
document given by US State Department officials to Secretary of State Lansing before a meeting of the so-called
Great Powers – France, Britain, the United States and Italy
– not only named the countries which in Washington's view
should be invited, but also gave the reasons in some cases
why certain nations should be included – or excluded. With
respect to Cuba, the authors accepted that the island state
was a 'minor and somewhat inactive belligerent', but added
that the country had 'identified herself with the policy of the
United States in the war and must, therefore, be included'.
Likewise for Panama, the briefing note pointed out that if the
planned treaty had provisions affecting the Panama Canal,
then it might 'very well claim a special interest which would
necessitate her inclusion, apart from her position as a minor
and inactive belligerent'. For the other four countries – Nicaragua, Honduras, Guatemala and Haiti – the reason for their
inclusion was rather more basic. 'Their position in the Peace
Conference would seem to be an interest of the United States
and consequently they should be signatures to the Treaty of
Peace,' the memo noted matter-of-factly. As for Costa Rica,

though it had declared war, it should not be invited 'for the reason that no government exists in that country which is recognised by the United States'.[3]

The composition of the Paris Peace Conference was still up in the air until just days before the formal opening. At a lengthy preliminary meeting of the four Great Powers that began at the French Foreign Ministry on 12 January, it fell to President Woodrow Wilson to emerge as the champion for the smaller nations – especially those from Latin America – to be fully represented at the Conference. He felt that just allowing smaller nations to attend those bits of the Conference that affected them – as the French were suggesting – would send out the wrong signals. The issue of representation was essentially one of 'sentiment and psychology', said the President; and his concern was that the 'Great Powers, to put the matter brutally, would appear to be running the Peace Conference'. At this point the British Prime Minister David Lloyd George archly remarked that it was the Great Powers who had run the war. The French Premier Georges Clemenceau was also concerned that the smaller powers would have too much say if they were given full representation. To illustrate his point the veteran politician singled out the proposed attendance of the Central American nations. Clemenceau asked 'whether he was to understand that no decision could be taken without Costa Rica and Honduras being consulted. If so, he could not agree [to this]. It was evident that in European questions the dangers were not so great for Costa Rica or Nicaragua as for European Powers...'[4]

In the end, a compromise that can best be characterised as a mixture of muddle and cynicism was agreed. President Wilson had already suggested that the peace process should consist of 'conversations' rather than 'formal Conferences',

PRESIDENT WILSON'S FOURTEEN POINTS, 8 JANUARY 1918

The program of the world's peace, therefore, is our program; and that program, the only possible program, as we see it, is this:

I. Open covenants of peace, openly arrived at, after which there shall be no private international understandings of any kind but diplomacy shall proceed always frankly and in the public view.

II. Absolute freedom of navigation upon the seas, outside territorial waters, alike in peace and in war, except as the seas may be closed in whole or in part by international action for the enforcement of international covenants.

III. The removal, so far as possible, of all economic barriers and the establishment of an equality of trade conditions among all the nations consenting to the peace and associating themselves for its maintenance.

IV. Adequate guarantees given and taken that national armaments will be reduced to the lowest point consistent with domestic safety.

V. A free, open-minded, and absolutely impartial adjustment of all colonial claims, based upon a strict observance of the principle that in determining all such questions of sovereignty the interests of the populations concerned must have equal weight with the equitable claims of the government whose title is to be determined.

VI. The evacuation of all Russian territory and such a settlement of all questions affecting Russia as will secure the best and freest cooperation of the other nations of the world in obtaining for her an unhampered and unembarrassed opportunity for the independent determination of her own political development and national policy and assure her of a sincere welcome into the society of free nations under institutions of her own choosing; and, more than a welcome, assistance also of every kind that she may need and may herself desire. The treatment accorded Russia by her sister nations in the months to come will be the acid test of their good will, of their comprehension of her needs as distinguished from their own interests, and of their intelligent and unselfish sympathy.

VII. Belgium, the whole world will agree, must be evacuated and restored, without any attempt to limit the sovereignty which she enjoys in common with all other free nations. No other single act will serve as this will serve to restore confidence among the nations in the laws which they have themselves set and determined for the government of their relations with one another. Without this healing act the whole structure and validity of international law is forever impaired.

VIII. All French territory should be freed and the invaded portions restored, and the wrong done to France by Prussia in 1871 in the matter of Alsace-Lorraine, which has unsettled the peace of the world for nearly fifty years, should be righted, in order that peace may once more be made secure in the interest of all.

IX. A readjustment of the frontiers of Italy should be effected along clearly recognizable lines of nationality.

X. The peoples of Austria-Hungary, whose place among the nations we wish to see safeguarded and assured, should be accorded the freest opportunity to autonomous development.

XI. Rumania, Serbia, and Montenegro should be evacuated; occupied territories restored; Serbia accorded free and secure access to the sea; and the relations of the several Balkan states to one another determined by friendly counsel along historically established lines of allegiance and nationality; and international guarantees of the political and economic independence and territorial integrity of the several Balkan states should be entered into.

XII. The Turkish portion of the present Ottoman Empire should be assured a secure sovereignty, but the other nationalities which are now under Turkish rule should be assured an undoubted security of life and an absolutely unmolested opportunity of autonomous development, and the Dardanelles should be permanently opened as a free passage to the ships and commerce of all nations under international guarantees.

XIII. An independent Polish state should be erected which should include the territories inhabited by indisputably Polish populations, which should be assured a free and secure access to the sea, and whose political and economic independence and territorial integrity should be guaranteed by international covenant.

XIV. A general association of nations must be formed under specific covenants for the purpose of affording mutual guarantees of political independence and territorial integrity to great and small states alike.

as the latter would only lead to the dissatisfaction of the smaller nations and 'satisfaction was an essential part of the Peace settlement'. Instead the Peace Conference was to have both; a formal set-piece conference at whose major gatherings little of substance was agreed, while behind the scenes in their own meetings the Great Powers would effectively dictate the agenda and the content of the subsequent treaties. As President Wilson had foreseen, this would lead to considerable dissatisfaction among some of the smaller powers. Initially, however, most were simply grateful to be invited. [5]

LATIN AMERICAN REPRESENTATION
Whether countries in Latin America were invited to participate in the Paris Peace Conference depended on their stance during the war. Those countries that had declared war on Germany were asked to attend; these were Brazil and the six Central American and Caribbean Republics under discussion. Those countries which had broken off relations with Germany were also invited: Bolivia, Ecuador, Peru and Uruguay. Neutral countries, including El Salvador in Central America, were not asked to take part.

As the weeks after the war ended dragged on, the Central American and Caribbean nations which had declared war grew increasingly concerned about whether they would receive an invitation to attend, perhaps unaware that the conference rules were being made up by the Great Powers as they went along. In early December, for example, the Panamanian representative in Madrid wrote to Lansing in Paris to enquire what the American thought he should do. In a poorly typed and spelt letter, Antonio Burgos informed Lansing that *I have been designed* [*sic*] *to represent my nation at the Peace Conference*, even though at that time it was by no means certain Panama would be asked to attend. Clearly trying to fish for information, and having reassured Lansing that his country wanted to reach agreement with the United States on all key issues likely to be raised at the Conference,

Burgos said, *You would ... oblige me very much by kindly informing me whether you think that my presence in Paris, before the opening of the Conference, would be of any use to you, or if ... it is better that I remain in Madrid until the Conference opens.* [6]

What Burgos almost certainly did not know was that while the Americans were very keen to have Panama at the Conference, they were far less happy at the choice of Burgos as the delegate. Indeed, they had been somewhat taken aback that he was the man chosen by Panama. Some weeks before, the American Minister in Panama, the assiduous Jennings Price, had dutifully given the State Department his assessment of the likely candidates to be the Panamanian representative in Paris were they to be asked to participate. In some detail he assessed the relative merits, marital status and background of each of the candidates who formed, in his judgement, the 'group from which selection will be made'. There were ten names on the list and it was a thorough piece of work. There was just one drawback: none of those on it was selected. Instead President Belisario Porras opted for Burgos. [7]

Perhaps because Price had singularly failed to predict the selection of Burgos, the diplomat was scathing in his assessment of the Panamanian. Announcing himself 'disappointed' with the choice, Price said that President Porras had plainly been motivated 'by a desire to award [*sic*] political friends' rather than choose someone of the 'standing' and 'qualification' that 'should characterise the representatives at this historic Conference'. According to the diplomat, Porras claimed his choice was motivated by the desire to 'save as much as possible the expense incurred in sending delegates' – hardly a convincing sign by Panama that it attached huge importance to the Peace Conference. Price informed his masters that while Burgos, a long-standing friend of Porras, 'will likely attempt to be fairly congenial with our representatives', he was 'not the man who measures up to the high standard suitable in this matter'. Warming to his task, Price continued, 'He is a smooth politician with scruples none too many, and an opportunist and a bargainer, according to the best judgements I have been able to form.' In fairness, the diplomat said he had already spoken in previous years to the State Department about Burgos' character. Price was also able to include a copy of a cable Burgos had sent to Panama on 4 December upon learning of his nomination as delegate. In it Burgos made clear that he *firmly* supported the *international policy of United States*, including the *Wilson proclamation* to *defend weak peoples* – presumably a reference to the plan for a League of Nations. Nor did Burgos neglect more practical matters. *Please send expenses*, he requested.[8]

> 'He is a smooth politician with scruples none too many, and an opportunist... .'
> AMERICAN DIPLOMAT ON ANTONIO BURGOS

Jennings Price was not alone in his low opinion of Antonio Burgos. Despite Burgos being quick off the mark with a letter to Lansing in December, and his cabling Panama for money, the Conference got under way in January without any sign of the Panamanian in Paris. The reason for this was that as late as the beginning of February the French authorities were still refusing him permission to enter the country. The Americans had learnt why: their man in Madrid where Burgos was based had been 'unofficially and confidentially informed that [the] French Intelligence Service has adverse information concerning Burgos'. What this 'adverse information' was is not clear, though a suggestion that it may have been connected with Burgos' supposed attitudes to the Allies is hinted at in the comments of the American diplomat in Madrid. He said that not only had he 'no confirmation' of the reports of Burgos' troubling views but 'on the contrary' his Embassy was of the opinion that 'Burgos is absolutely loyal'. Burgos professed himself baffled as to why he was being refused an entry visa and in a letter to the American Embassy in Madrid he expressed both his anger and frustration. The *obstacles* put forward by a *country which is a loyal friend* [France] more *than mortify me*, he wrote. In fact they made him *feel like renouncing the position of delegate to the Conference of Peace.*[9]

The issue of Burgos' visa was considered important enough to be raised at a meeting of the United States conference delegation on 7 February, where it was decided that 'no action should be taken'. According to minutes of that meeting Lansing said he knew Burgos and that 'he personally distrusted him'. The memo continued: '[Lansing] felt that he was only a politician, and that in the interest of Panama it might almost be advisable to have another peace Delegate sent to Paris.' Thus the Americans would not take any action 'unless we were actually approached by the government of Panama'. But there was 'no objection' to asking the State Department to 'make an investigation into the standing and reputation of Mr Burgos' if this was felt necessary. However, shortly after the memo was written Burgos was at last allowed to travel to Paris to take up his position. Nonetheless, question marks over the Panamanian's character did not entirely go away. In late May Jennings Price was once again airing his views about Burgos, at the specific request of the State Department – suggesting that it did belatedly carry out an 'investigation' into the delegate's 'standing'. Price reiterated much of what he had said before, adding, 'He is not believed to be anti-American but is considered a rather unscrupulous politician ... .' Price pointed out that Burgos had been in his country's diplomatic and consular service in Italy and Spain for fifteen years and in that time had made just three brief visits back to Panama. 'He does not enjoy high standing or regard in Panama, being considered rather undependable,' added the American.[10]

The choice of delegates made by the other Central American and Caribbean countries did not cause as many headaches for the Great Powers as the selection of Burgos. Potentially the most troubling for the Allies was that made by Honduras. Policarpo Bonilla was a bold choice for President Bertrand. Bonilla was a colourful and well-known character who had not only been President of his country – which he ruled as a dictator – but had also been implicated in a number of plots against governments he opposed there, and had spent time in prison in Tegucigalpa. Moreover, Bonilla had carried out much of his scheming on American soil in New Orleans and was not noted for being pro-United States. At the same time, however, he was a big hitter for President Bertrand to send. A gifted orator, Bonilla enjoyed the status of having been a President and also had extensive contacts across Central America. This was partly because of his still burning desire to see the region united once more politically. In fact, not only did the Americans have no objection to Bonilla coming to Paris on behalf of Honduras, he was, curiously, described as 'friendly to the U.S.'. However Bonilla was determined that once at the Conference he would not simply make up the numbers. In particular, he was keen to raise an issue that had been hanging over the region for many years – what exactly the Monroe Doctrine meant for Latin American countries.[11]

In the case of Guatemala, it had hoped to send a senior Minister, Dr Luis Toledo Herrarte, a former representative of his country in Washington and Foreign Minister, and so he was named as the country's delegate. Having worked in the United States he was someone the Americans knew they could do business with. However, for reasons that are unclear, Herrarte was unable to travel to Paris, and instead his place was taken by Joaquín Méndez, who was Guatemala's Minister in Washington. Though technically not such a big name as Herrarte, Méndez was nonetheless a shrewd choice by the wily President Cabrera. The diplomat, who was married to an American, had been in Washington since before the start of the war, and like Herrarte knew his way around the State Department and its personnel. He was thus also a reassuringly familiar figure for Guatemala's key ally at the conference, the United States. By choosing first Herrarte, then Méndez, the Guatemalan President was sending a very clear and reassuring message to the American delegates that his country did not intend to rock the boat in Paris. Having joined the war out of pragmatic self-interest, Cabrera was determined that the Americans would have every reason to 'reward' his conciliatory behaviour. The Americans were well aware of Guatemalan intentions. Having heard about Herrarte's original nomination as a delegate, Lansing remarked admiringly that 'President Cabrera was undoubtedly the ablest politician in Central America and knew how to play the game beautifully'. The overall diplomatic assessment of Méndez, meanwhile, was 'very sympathetic to U.S.'. [12]

The French, however, probably felt they had good reason not to be overjoyed at the presence of anyone from Guatemala at the Conference. Towards the end of the war France had awarded President Estrada Cabrera the Grand Croix de la Légion d'Honneur and also handed the Croix d'Officier to an official. Officially this was done to reward Guatemala for its stance in joining the Allies; unofficially it was to encourage the regime to check German economic activity in the country – namely its coffee owners – and boost France's trade prospects in the future. Yet soon afterwards Estrada Cabrera appointed a man called A. Matos as one of his diplomats in France. French intelligence officials were convinced that Matos had Hungarian citizenship and would spy for the Central Powers from his Parisian vantage point. The French authorities felt the Guatemalan dictator had shown little honour in the episode, a feeling not helped by the fact that they were also convinced Estrada Cabrera had property worth up to $20 million in Hamburg and Frankfurt.[13]

When Nicaraguan President Emiliano Chamorro came to decide who would represent his country in Paris, he stayed close to home. By choosing his own father Salvador Chamorro, President Chamorro was getting an experienced politician who knew his way round Central American politics – he was speaker of the Nicaraguan House of Deputies – and one who could be relied upon to carry out the government's bidding without question. At the time, the Nicaraguan government was making a concerted effort to pay off its foreign debt and thus needed the cooperation of the large creditor nations sitting around the conference table in Paris. But Salvador Chamorro had his own, rather more personal and tragic reason for wanting to be in Paris. Another of his sons had volunteered to serve with the French as a surgeon but had died while on duty. The Americans were certainly pleased – but perhaps not wholly surprised – to see a country that they effectively controlled as a protectorate choose such a suitable representative. 'Very friendly to U.S. and supports all U.S. policies,' was the satisfied verdict of American diplomats on Salvador Chamorro.[14]

Meanwhile the selection of the delegates of Haiti and Cuba apparently raised little reaction at all among the Americans. The choice of Tertulien Guilbaud was a logical one for the Haitian authorities, as the French-speaker was already the Haitian Minister to France and was also a significant figure in his country's political landscape. As for the Cubans, they chose a renowned lawyer in Antonio Sánchez de Bustamante rather than a more high-profile political figure. Bustamante's forte was in fine print and legal details, and he was perhaps thus not regarded as someone likely to rock the diplomatic boat. Moreover, as the foreign policies of both Haiti and Cuba were so firmly under the control of the United States, it was doubtless felt that the identity of their delegates was not of the first importance.

The Central American and Caribbean delegates were not sent to the Conference without backup. Though their countries were only allowed one accredited representative, each of the countries had support staff. For example Cuba's Bustamante not only had a technical advisor, he also had a secretariat of six people helping the mission, including the country's Minister in France, Guillermo de Blanck. Guatemala's Mendez had three people in his secretariat, including a military attaché, a Captain Miguel Idigoras from the country's military academy. Haiti, probably the poorest of the region's countries present, had two people in the secretariat to assist Tertulien Guilbaud, while Nicaragua's Chamorro had four staff, including a lawyer. Only Policarpo Bonilla of Honduras was not formally accredited with any support staff. In the case of Panama, Burgos had two members in his secretariat plus two technical advisors – one of them a serving soldier. Lieutenant-Colonel Arthur Budd was a member of the American Army. Nor was he an American stooge foisted upon an unwilling Panama. In fact Burgos had taken the trouble to contact the American Ambassador in Paris Henry White to see if the Americans had any objection to Budd – who was with the 311th Infantry Regiment – being attached to its delegation. White had no problem with this and Burgos expressed his gratitude. There was just one snag, though, and that was that the Panamanian had been trying to contact the officer without success. ... *I would be very grateful if you could help me to find the spot where Colonel Budd is*, wrote Burgos. Though the delegates had backup teams, not all of them were able to attend the opening weeks of the Conference however. For example, Méndez only left the United States for Paris aboard the *Rochambeau* on 5 March. In a cable to the State Department in Washington in late February, meanwhile, the American delegation was still anxiously trying to find out the name of the Honduran delegate – they were at that time unaware that it was to be Policarpo Bonilla. Nor was Cuba's Bustamante immediately on hand for the start of the international gathering. Thus all three men were missing from the list of attendees for the opening meeting on 18 January.[15]

A delegate from Costa Rica, meanwhile, would never make it to the Conference at all. On 13 January the American delegation in Paris received a cable from Washington outlining 'reliable reports' that the Tinoco regime in Costa Rica was using its Minister in Paris, Manuel de Peralta, to try to get the country admitted to the Peace Conference. This sent alarm bells ringing; the Americans were determined that Costa Rica should not be allowed in because the US did not recognise the regime. Woodrow Wilson himself raised the issue at a meeting of the Great Powers on 13 January, presumably in a bid to forestall Costa Rica's lobbying. Wilson told the other leaders, 'Tinoco had hastened to declare war on Germany after the United States had done so for the sole purpose of obtaining recognition, and that he [Wilson] felt he could not afford to associate with a representative of Costa Rica at the Peace Conference.' Given Britain's indifference to the participation of any Central American nations, it was hardly surprising that it raised little objection to this and it was agreed. France, on the other hand, was sympathetic to Costa Rica's case. But as Peralta soon realised, France was not prepared to do battle with Woodrow Wilson over Costa Rica, as it had far more pressing matters to consider. The Costa Rican was also disdainful of what he called the 'absolute adulation' the Allies had for the 'idol' Wilson.[16]

However, the Allies' decision on 13 January was not quite the end of the matter, as the Tinoco brothers and Peralta were determined not to give up. Their man in Paris sent the Great Powers' leaders a detailed summary of what Costa Rica felt was its strong case. In a covering letter Peralta said his country had 'spared no sacrifice' in favour of the Allies and had met its obligations as a nation at war 'despite the enormous economic and financial difficulties' caused to it by the conflict. He also pointed out that a French newspaper *Le Temps* had, on 15 January, named Costa Rica as one of the countries that would take part in the international gathering. And yet, said the Costa Rican diplomat, the country had been alone among the Latin American countries which broke relations or declared war on the Central Powers in not being invited. 'The Government of Costa Rica does not know the reasons for its exclusion and this unfair treatment seems to it as strange as it is unjustified, especially when considering the profession of principles made by the Allies: liberty and equality for all peoples, great and small, all equal before justice and law.' Once again there was a little disquiet among the American diplomatic corps. Measures were taken to try to find out what the French and other leading countries present thought of the request. Ultimately, however, Costa Rica's plea fell on deaf ears and the Conference duly continued without it.[17]

Though most of the Central American and Caribbean states who did make it to the Conference were mainly happy just to be present at such an august gathering – the eagerness to be there underlined by Costa Rica's frantic efforts to gain access – this did not mean they were entirely devoid of their own demands and agendas. Yes, the chance to rub shoulders with the Great Powers and perhaps boost trade opportunities was a huge bonus for these countries. But they also had particular issues they wanted to raise or at least follow closely. An important matter and one common to all of the six was the formation of the proposed League of Nations.

The planned League at this point meant different things to different parts of the world. For the Europeans – and especially the French – it either meant a chance to guarantee themselves from future attacks from Germany or it meant nothing at all. For its instigator Woodrow Wilson it was intended to be a mechanism for resolving conflicts around the world and thus avoid the United States being dragged into more faraway wars. But for Latin American countries, and particularly nations in Central America and the Caribbean, it was not German aggression or possible future European wars that most concerned them. Their priority was to have a safeguard against American intervention, something that had been seen with increasing regularity in the last two decades.

For the Central American and Caribbean nations the issues of the League and the Monroe Doctrine were intimately connected. The Monroe Doctrine may have protected the smaller states from European aggression, but did it protect them from American actions? The so-called Roosevelt Corollary and recent events suggested not. However a League of Nations, by whose rules the United States would be bound, could potentially provide that protection, a possibility not lost on the region's politicians. They wanted to take Wilson at his word and, in a sense to hoist him with his own petard. Wilson's plan was to protect the interests of weaker nations, and, as far as regional leaders were concerned, that meant Central American and Caribbean countries too. This was an issue whose importance – and potential for mischief towards the United States – was not lost on Costa Rica's Peralta when he realised that his country was to be denied admission to the Conference. In a parting shot to those Latin American representatives who were invited, he suggested they insist on a clause in the Peace Treaty that would provide a check to the Monroe Doctrine as interpreted by Washington.[18]

Peralta's exhortation was probably not necessary. An eagerness to exploit Wilson's words and play the American President at his own game was already present on the part of Panama's government. President Belisario Porras betrayed some impatience with his Paris delegate and friend Antonio Burgos when the latter had cabled back home stating, *I firmly support international policy of United States. Practical application with respect to defence of weak peoples as in Wilson proclamation.* 'I see that you are imbued with ideas of democracy, of the revindication of the humble, of the justification of the downtrodden, and of the redemption of the exploited and oppressed. Good for you, Don Antonio,' wrote President Porras. 'But the important thing is to sustain these ideas in practice and make them effective in the Congress.'[19]

The President then went on to explain what he meant by 'in practice', at the same time revealing the lingering bitterness that still existed in Panama over the terms of the treaty in which they ceded authority of the Canal Zone to Washington and over the actions of their large neighbour to the north. 'It is necessary to obtain that the United States treat us with more consideration that they have been treating us so far, particularly lately,' urged President Porras, doubtless unaware that the letter would be intercepted and read by the American delegation in Paris. He then referred to the document signed to create the Canal Zone. 'Above all we must change the present treaty which was made as Sr. Buneau-Varilla [the Frenchman who signed it on the country's behalf in 1903] himself confesses in a book ... almost at midnight.' Porras insisted that the current situation was different from the time when the treaty was signed, which thus justified the modification of many of its clauses. This was the case, he argued, as 'it is impossible, morally and politically speaking, to conserve our independence which the United States guarantees, if the same American Government, with the right to take our lands and water appropriates both whenever it desires without justifying the necessity and without paying us any indemnity.' [20]

President Porras gave Burgos the concrete example of the Panamanian island of Taboga, which he said the Americans had attempted to occupy – though this action had been 'suspended for the present' – under the pretext of building fortifications to defend the Canal. 'The loss of our best island ... in order to place cannons thereon at the very time at which peace is dawning and they are attempting to establish the League of Nations, and of the, as you say "the revindication of the humble, the justification of the downtrodden, and of the redemption of the exploited and oppressed", is very significant.' Interestingly, Porras finished his letter by urging Burgos to 'link yourself closely' with the delegates from

Brazil 'and other, Spanish-American, nations which may lend us their aid'.[21]

Perhaps stung by the tone of his President's letter, Burgos made sure that, when the occasion arose, he did not miss the chance to outline his country's views on the need for the independence and sovereignty of smaller nations to be guaranteed. His moment came on 28 April when a meeting of the Plenary Conference was held to approve the Covenant of the League of Nations, which would form part of the Versailles Treaty. The Plenary Conference consisted of all delegates and was essentially a talking shop whose purpose was to rubber-stamp decisions and documents already agreed in smaller committees that were either dominated by or consisted entirely of the Great Powers. Thus none of the speakers on 28 April had any realistic chance of changing the Covenant. It was, though, a good place to let off steam or simply to put views on the diplomatic record. It was an opportunity that Antonio Burgos seized.

Speaking in French, Burgos outlined why his country was backing the new League, his lengthy remarks later filling up six full pages of the official minutes of the meeting. Aware that his country had perhaps received little attention at the Conference, the diplomat gave his fellow delegates a little taste of recent history regarding Panama. *It is a small State, but its people, steeped in ideas of justice and liberty, was the first one in America, after the Republic of the United States, to adhere to the cause of the Allies*, he noted. *This people, at a moment when others stood silent and trembling before the injustice of the strong ... this people of Panama ...has always had confidence in the strength of the spirit which no human power can conquer... by which I mean Right, fighting literally to the death, but never yielding.* Going further back into history, Burgos said that his *satisfaction in being present at such important discussions* was made greater by the thought that it was at the Congress of Panama (in 1826) that Simón Bolívar had first suggested the idea of an institution that should group *together the American Republics to form the most immense, the most extraordinary, and the strongest League which has yet appeared on the earth.* [22]

> This people, at a moment when others stood silent and trembling before the injustice of the strong ... this people of Panama ... has always had confidence in the strength of the spirit which no human power can conquer... .
>
> **ANTONIO BURGOS, 1919**

Aware of his American audience, after praising the hero of Spanish America, Bolívar, Burgos quoted with approval remarks from the hero of North American liberation, George Washington. Then, referring to the League and its creator, the Panamanian remarked: *Do we not find in these remembrances something of the thought of President Wilson? ... he suggests the formation of a League of Nations, thanks to which troubles between States will disappear, democratic institutions will develop on normal lines, peoples will abandon all ideas of conquest and, by being certain that their rights will be respected, will no longer have cause to fear the domination of a formidably organised military power.* [23]

Yet as well as the lofty praise and the rather overblown rhetoric, Burgos speech contained a theme close to the hearts of both Panama and the other states in the region. That was the absolute right of all states to have their sovereignty respected. Burgos attacked those who claimed that being part of the collective framework of the League of Nations in some way reduced a country's sovereignty or independence.

… the Covenant of the League of Nations does not threaten the existence or independence of any … nations, he insisted. *Its exact purpose is to guarantee the existence of and independence of each one of them … .* In case the Americans did not get the message – that the rights of less powerful nations should be protected – Burgos was even more explicit soon afterwards when discussing the importance of arbitration in international disputes. *In the formation of nationalities it sometimes happens that a small State borders on a greater Power; how would that small State have the certainty of securing a hearing for its rights unless assured of the possibility of submitting to an arbitral tribunal such questions as might arise from its state of neighbourhood?* The delegates of all the nations of Central America and the Caribbean present would have readily identified with that 'small state'. The one thing, Burgos said, that should be withheld from the control of the League was the *independence or sovereignty of a people.* [24]

Finally, addressing the delegates of the larger nations, Burgos made a plea on behalf of all less powerful nations in which he effectively admitted that, without the help of institutions such as the League, they could do little. *Peoples like the one which I have the honor to represent which is small in … territory but great by the nobility of its aspirations … can live only through justice. It is at your hands that those peoples await the realization of their hopes, and you will have merited their eternal gratitude.*[25]

The assembled delegates had hardly had a chance to digest Burgos's lengthy remarks when another Central American representative addressed them. Unlike his Panamanian counterpart, Policarpo Bonilla chose to speak in Spanish rather than in French. Also unlike Burgos, who had dealt mostly in generalities, the Honduran had a more specific matter to raise

– the Monroe Doctrine. After considerable disagreement between the Americans and the French, it had been agreed that Article 21 of the Covenant should refer by name to the Monroe Doctrine, making clear that nothing in the Covenant should be deemed to 'affect the validity' of existing treaties or 'regional understandings like the Monroe Doctrine'. However, the Article did not spell out what was meant by the Doctrine. If it was a 'regional understanding', who precisely in the region understood what it meant? Bonilla insisted – as Costa Rica's Peralta had suggested – this be clarified in the form of an addition to Article 21. *The Monroe Doctrine directly affects the Latin American Republics; but since it has never been alluded to in any international document, nor been expressly accepted by the nations, either of the old continent or the new, and as it has been defined and applied in different ways by the statesmen and Presidents of the United States of America, I think it is necessary that it should be defined with absolute clearness in the Treaty ...* Bonilla declared. The former Honduran President said that in the absence of any explicit explanation given in the Covenant, the definition that the Article's authors surely had in mind was that given in recent speeches by President Woodrow Wilson. *... he laid it down that the Doctrine is not a menace but a guarantee for the weaker States of America, and he expressly disavowed the interpretations which had been given to it in the sense that it implies a kind of tutelage which the United States have the right to exercise over the remaining American Republics,* said Bonilla. In particular, in a speech to Mexican journalists on 7 June 1918, Wilson had stated that the guarantee implied in the Doctrine protecting the *weaker countries* from attack did not just apply to the *nations of the Old World* but also to the United States as well, said the Honduran.[26]

Policarpo Bonilla said he hoped that in these circumstances, his proposed addition to the Covenant would get a
kindly welcome from the United States delegation. However,
in seeking to define the Monroe Doctrine Bonilla was not just
concerned with protecting individual states from Old World
and United States aggression. For many years the veteran
Liberal had been a champion of Central American unity, and
this was an ideal that still burned brightly for him. So, faced
with such an august audience, Bonilla could not resist referring to his country's constitution, which gave it the *right …
of uniting with one or more of the nations of the Central
American Isthmus for the purpose of reconstituting what
was formerly the Republic of Central America.* Such a union,
he insisted, constituted the *finest ideal of patriotism in that
part of the world.*[27]

Bonilla's proposed amendment also referred to the right of
Latin American countries *confederating or otherwise uniting
themselves.* However its main thrust in defining the Monroe
Doctrine was to emphasise the rights of individual nations.
The amendment read: 'This doctrine, which has been supported by the United States of America since 1823 … means
that all the Republics of America have the right to an independent existence, and that no nation can there acquire by
conquest any portion of their territory nor intervene in their
internal government or administration, nor perform there
any act which can diminish their autonomy or wound their
national dignity.' It was obvious that this wording would have
forbidden all the interventions that the United States had
carried out in recent years, in Haiti, Cuba and Nicaragua.
This fact would not have been lost on either the United States
delegation in the hall or the various delegates present from
Central and South America and the Caribbean, who broadly

supported the proposed wording. There is however not the slightest indication that the amendment was ever seriously considered by the Great Powers, as Bonilla himself almost certainly knew would be the case. Indeed, the next speaker was French Minister Stephen Pichon, who immediately moved the discussion onto other matters. The United States delegation, which had enough difficulties back in Washington over the extent to which the League would be a shackle on foreign policy, had no intention of getting drawn into a definition of the Monroe Doctrine that could only further inflame opinion back home.[28]

5

Unhappy in Paris

Important though the League of Nations was to the smaller nations, lofty international issues were not the only matters that the six countries were determined to raise in Paris. Some issues involved purely domestic affairs that, in theory at least, had little to do with the war that had just ended or the making of the peace. Yet for a small country such as Haiti the possibility of having real discussions with the President of the United States and its Secretary of State rather than simply dealing with American representatives based on the island was too good to miss. Accordingly, the country's Foreign Minister Constantin Benoit sent a shopping list of items, big and small, that he wanted Haiti's representative in Paris, the versatile diplomat-politician-poet Tertulien Guilbaud, to raise during the Conference.

Top of the list were demands aimed at Germany. However, the first of these arose not from the war but dated back to 1897 and the Luders Affair (discussed in Chapter 2), when Berlin's gunboat diplomacy on the island had caused such an affront to Haitian pride. Benoit requested that Guilbaud raise Haiti's demand for the $20,000 that Germany had 'exacted of us' in December 1897, plus interest, following the 'brutal abuse of power of which Germany was guilty in acting against us'. Next on the list was compensation for the families of Haitians killed on board the merchant ships *Montreal* and *Karnak* when they were sunk by German submarines in 1916. Benoit was particularly annoyed at the way that Berlin had reacted to the claims at the time of the sinkings. 'Germany responded ... by handing his [the Chargé d'Affaires'] passports to our Charge [*sic*] d'Affaires,' he wrote. He also reminded the country's man in Paris that it was the Legation there that had first alerted the Haitian government to the sinkings in January and June 1917; '... you ought ... therefore to have in your possession all necessary information to press these claims'.[1]

Benoit next raised with Guilbaud two cases of Haitian citizens who claimed to have suffered at the hands of the Germans during the war. One was a Eugene Pescay who had been living in northern France when the Germans invaded. '... [he was] carried away into captivity, and subjected to absolutely inhuman treatment at the hands of the German authorities,' wrote Benoit, adding that the 'barbarous proceedings of which he was victim' occurred before Haiti had broken off relations with Germany. 'You will ... put in a claim for damages in favor of that Haitian citizen,' the Foreign Minister instructed Guilbaud. The second case involved a Mr Mackenzie, another Haitian, who on 6 February 1914 had sent a consignment of 140 bags of coffee to a merchant at Le Havre, which was then sent on to Antwerp where it was kept in a warehouse. In the meantime, the Germans had invaded and, said Benoit, despite representations made by the Haitian authorities, Mackenzie had neither got back the coffee nor received any money for it. 'We are sending you copies of all documents concerning this case so that you can intelligently support the just claims of our compatriot,' wrote the Foreign Minister.[2]

Last, but certainly not least, Benoit said he was 'entrusting' Guilbaud to undertake what he described as a 'special mission' on behalf of the country in relation to President Wilson and Secretary of State Lansing. For Haiti, like Panama, was unhappy at the way it was being treated by the United States and saw the Conference as an ideal opportunity to put that right. In particular, the Haitian authorities, already frustrated at their lack of autonomy after the United States' intervention in 1915, were aggrieved at what one official called the 'vexatious and unfair tyranny of American officials'. The special mission concerned two key issues. First was the 'Abolition, in Haiti, of the regime of Martial Law and of the Provost Courts instituted since the arrival of the American Occupation in Haiti, the continuation of which is no longer justifiable.' The second was the recognition of the right of the Haitian government under the 1915 Convention with the United States to 'appoint and revoke the Haitian employees of all the Customs Houses of the Republic'. This second issue, said Benoit, 'has never received any solution in spite of its great importance to us'.[3]

The Foreign Minister went on to explain how he wanted Guilbaud to proceed – and why he wanted to use the Peace Conference to press issues that were unconnected with the aftermath of the war in Europe. 'You will see [President Wilson and Secretary of State Lansing] personally,' instructed Benoit. 'We have preferred to adopt this course because it seemed to us the most likely one to produce practical results. As a matter of fact, it will be easier for you to arrive at the solution of the difficulty by addressing yourself personally to President Wilson and to his Secretary of State who, we believe, have not always been faithfully informed by their agents in Haiti on what was passing here.' In having what Benoit hoped would be a 'heart-to-heart conversation' with the two men, it was more likely that Guilbaud could 'obtain justice' in these two matters.[4]

In his instructions to Guilbaud, Benoit also showed that he had a good grasp of the finer points of diplomacy, by making it clear that the 'special mission' issues should be raised bilaterally rather than on the Conference floor itself. 'We believe that the American government will be better disposed to admit our claims if we seek for their solution in a tête-à-tête than if we took the matter before the Peace Conference.' He said that perhaps the Americans might think they would win the case against Haiti in a public discussion. But, Benoit argued, '…just at the moment when their Chief, President Wilson, is saying that one of the principal reasons for his personal presence at the table of the Conference is to assure the acceptance of the principle of respect for the rights of smaller nations by the greater, the representatives of the American government, President Wilson himself, Mr Lansing, who knows how often we have laid our claims before him without obtaining justice, should surely deem it best, at this hour, that the voice of a feeble nation like Haiti should not be heard in the assembly of nations to justly complain of the injustice suffered at the hands of the powerful republic of the United States.' In other words, Washington would realise that if it did not agree privately to these demands, they might face being described as hypocrites in the Conference. Like Panama, Haiti was hoping to use Wilson's own rhetoric about the need to defend weaker nations against him to press their claims.[5]

Finally, Benoit said that while Guilbaud should get as

close as possible to the American delegation, he should not neglect other countries, so that 'if, on certain questions, the United States should fail to support you, we can, for instance, depend on that of France and England', He ended: 'Keep a close watch over, best so as to reap, if needs be, all the advantages possible for our country ... the Government relies ... upon your tact, your clairvoyance and your skill.'

Though Guilbaud was an experienced diplomat and politician, there was a considerable level of expectation being heaped upon his shoulders. Nor did Guilbaud have the benefit of surprise when pressing his country's claims on the American delegation. Once again the United States spy network had been at work and a 'Colonel Russell' – presumably American Colonel John H Russell who was brigade commander in Port-au-Prince – had 'confidentially' handed over a copy of Benoit's letter to the State Department at the start of March. Yet again the Americans knew the bargaining position of another country almost as well as its own delegate.[6]

In fact even without the 'leak', the Americans would hardly have been surprised to learn of Haiti's unhappiness over martial law and, above all, over the lack of control over its own finances through the Customs House. Throughout the second half of 1918 the Haitian government under President Philippe Sudre Dartiguenave had been at loggerheads with local American officials, particular when he appointed a new and more assertive Finance Minister, Louis Borno. So assertive was Borno, indeed, that Colonel Russell and the American Minister in Haiti Arthur Bailly-Blanchard felt obliged to demand the President remove him from office – which he duly did. Dartiguenave then sought to lobby Washington more directly through the Haitian Legation there. After months of no reply, the Haitians eventually received a curt rejection.

Thus the decision to use Guilbaud in Paris was the third initiative on the issue tried out by the hard-pressed and increasingly cash-starved Haitian government.

Guilbaud dutifully went to see Lansing in Paris and at first it seemed as if the erudite poet's approach and Benoit's shrewd tactics might bear fruit. Lansing quickly saw the merit in avoiding negative publicity about alleged American bullying of a smaller nation even as President Wilson was championing the minnows' cause so vigorously in the Conference rooms of Paris. He suggested to the State Department that at the time when the Peace Treaty in Paris was signed it would be a good idea to downgrade the marine brigade in Port-au-Prince into a 'legation guard'. However, officials in Haiti and Acting Secretary of State Frank Polk – he was fulfilling all non-Peace Conference related duties – rejected the idea. At the time Haiti was facing an internal revolt, and the marines were being called on to help the local gendarmerie suppress it.[7]

Guilbaud's failure to shift American policy in Haiti was hardly a surprise, given the lack of success in previous attempts by President Dartiguenave. Nor was it to be the only setback or failure for Central American and Caribbean countries at the peace talks. The problems that these countries faced in getting their voices heard individually has led to suggestions that the Latin Americans at the Conference – the six Central American and Caribbean states plus Brazil, Bolivia, Peru, Ecuador and Uruguay – operated as a form of unofficial regional lobby group. As we have already seen, there was certainly an eagerness on the part of countries such as Panama to cooperate with neighbours from the region, with Brazil – the biggest and most powerful of the Latin American countries present – seen as the natural leader of any such grouping. However, the evidence is mixed as to whether a genuine Latin American bloc emerged, still less that there was a 'smaller powers' bloc including other countries from outside the region.

An early and non-controversial opportunity to show Latin American solidarity came quite early in proceedings when the French Prime Minister Georges Clemenceau was shot and wounded on 19 February. The attack happened as the veteran politician left his home to meet President Wilson's adviser Colonel House and the British delegate Arthur Balfour. The assailant jumped out and fired seven shots at the car in which Clemenceau was sitting. Fortunately for the 'Tiger', as he was nicknamed, just one shot hit its target and even this one somehow managed to miss all the premier's vital organs. Clemenceau was walking within a day and back at his desk within a week. But though he played down the shooting, the attack shook both him and world opinion. The spectre of communism – some initially wrongly thought that it might be a Bolshevik-inspired attack – was already hanging over the Conference. Many feared that Germany, bitterly divided by its defeat, could itself fall to Bolshevism. The attempt on Clemenceau's life made the prospect of unrest and turmoil seem very close to Peace Conference delegates in Paris.

Representatives from various Latin American delegations got together to send a telegram to Clemenceau's house. The telegram, sent on 20 February, expressed their 'profound sympathy' and their 'indignation' at the attempt on his life, and wished him a 'quick and complete recovery'. It was signed by Guilbaud for Haiti, Burgos for Panama and Bustamante for Cuba, as well as by other Latin American delegates. It is not clear if the delegates for Honduras, Guatemala and Nicaragua had also sent their own messages. A reply made on Clemenceau's behalf indicates that the politician was touched by the gesture. 'I ask you to communicate to all the Latin American representatives his feelings of deep gratitude,' it read.[8]

However, the real evidence for a Latin American bloc – if such it was – came over an issue that probably created the most discontent among the smaller states at the Conference and which even led some of them to threaten to walk out. This was the question of who should be represented on which Conference Commission.

The organisation of the Conference was a complicated affair. As well as the Plenary Conference which included all delegates – and which met infrequently – and the Cabinet Office of the Great Powers that ran the gathering, there was also a series of Commissions. These were set up to tackle a range of specific issues, from those that arose directly from the war, such as war crimes, to those looking ahead to wider concerns, such as the Commission on International Labour Legislation. Membership of these Commissions – many of which ended up making little progress – was dominated by delegates from the major nations. But the smaller countries wanted their say, too, and a meeting of the so-called Powers with Special Interests – that is the smaller states – was created to decide how they should be represented on the Commissions.

The first of these meetings was held on 27 January 1919 and was chaired by French diplomat Jules Cambon. Its purpose was to work out the representation of the smaller powers on four Commissions: those on the League of Nations, ports, international labour legislation and war crimes. How many of them should be on each Commission was something that had already been decided by the Great Powers. There would be ten delegates from the latter group on each body, with the smaller powers having just five. Cambon's task was simply to get them to agree which five smaller powers should be represented on each Commission.

The meeting – conducted in French – went smoothly and eventually the smaller powers present agreed to vote among themselves on how to carve up the Commission slots. Just two of the six Central American and Caribbean states were represented at this gathering. Haiti was represented by Tertulien Guilbaud, who as Minister to Paris for his country was already in France. Cuba's man at the meeting was Rafael Martinez Ortiz, also a Paris-based diplomat; Bustamante had not yet arrived. The other four countries were not represented for a variety of reasons; some, such as Guatemala, had scarcely chosen their delegate yet, while Panama's Burgos was still trying to gain entry to the country.

Though this initial meeting passed off without major discord, there were signs that some of the countries were displeased about the decisions being taken in advance by the Great Powers on Commission membership size. In particular, the Brazilian delegation made it clear that it was unhappy that membership of all the Commissions and especially the one on the League of Nations – the one issue which clearly affected all countries – was being restricted in this way. One of its delegates, Pandia Calogeras, told Cambon that the principle of the League had already been agreed, and that it should be one nation, one vote. 'That is the spirit in which I beg leave to bring to your attention the arguments which appear to mitigate in favour of an increase in the number of members of commissions, for the phrase "League of Nations" must not merely appear in our speeches; its spirit must live in our hearts,' he said.[9]

Though the smaller powers accepted at this January meeting that they could not amend the number of Commission members, Calogeras and others had sent a warning message that they would not simply quietly acquiesce in all decisions made by the larger nations. Indeed, once the League of Nations Commission met, the smaller powers succeeded in having their representation increased from five to nine, though Brazil remained the only Latin American representative. The 27 January meeting also gave an early sign that Latin American states were cooperating in a way that they rarely did back home. Thus, when potential places came up on some of the less contentious Commissions, there nearly always seemed to be an agreed candidate from the Americas. Indeed, when the Belgian delegate told the chairman that the powers had agreed on candidates for the Commission on International Legislation on Labour he put forward the names 'Belgium, Serbia, Cuba for the South American [sic] group, Poland and the Czechoslovak Republic'. This was a notable success for the Cuban delegation, whose representative Bustamante – yet to arrive – would prove a useful member thanks to his legal expertise.[10]

By the time of a later meeting of the 'Powers with Special Interest' held on 3 March to discuss the membership of the important Economic and Financial Commissions, Antonio Burgos had finally arrived to represent Panama. The mood among smaller powers, meanwhile, had hardened considerably. The head of the Brazilian delegation, Epitácio Pessoa – who would shortly be elected President of his country – revealed to Jules Cambon that these states had already met in advance and come to the view that their membership on these Commissions had to be increased from five to ten. It would be 'impossible' otherwise for them to 'satisfy the just requirements of their situation', said Pessoa. He tabled a resolution urging that Cambon ask the Great Powers to reconsider their decision on membership numbers. The Frenchman was reluctant to follow Pessoa's suggestions and both the Greek and Belgian delegates backed the chairman's compromise suggestion that the smaller powers should vote for their five Commission members, and in addition, supply a list of extra names in case the Great Powers should see fit to extend their representation.[11]

In fact the smaller powers ultimately decided to vote on a list of ten representatives for each of the two Commissions being discussed, reserving to themselves, rather than the Great Powers, the right to trim this number back to five if the bigger countries failed to increase smaller ones' membership from five to ten. The Latin American countries were very well represented on these lists. Bolivia, Peru and Brazil were chosen as candidates for the Economics Commission, and Ecuador and Brazil for the Financial Commission, though none of the Central American or Caribbean states featured at this point. The smaller powers, frustrated at their lack of influence in Paris, had thrown down the gauntlet to the likes of Clemenceau, Lloyd George and Wilson.

However, if these states simply expected the bigger countries quietly to give way, they were to be disappointed. The Supreme Allied Council (made up of the US, France, Britain, Italy and Japan) quickly dismissed their claim and insisted that 'Powers with Special Interests' should be restricted to just five members on each of the two Commissions. So, on 6 March, the smaller powers met yet again, this time to whittle their list of chosen representatives down from ten to five. It was now that cracks began to appear not just between the smaller countries and the dominant powers, but within the ranks of the smaller states themselves. This was largely caused by the Latin Americans who were by now clearly operating as a bloc. The main coordinators of this Latin American caucus were Pessoa from Brazil and Ecuador's Enrique Dorn y de Alsúa.

The European powers were by now beginning to show signs of irritation with Latin American tactics. As the Greek delegate Nikolaos Politis diplomatically put it, during attempts to agree on Commission membership, the smaller powers had come up against a 'tendency on the part of the Latin American Powers to acquire more seats than they could obtain through an objective distribution which took European interests likewise into account'. When it came to the new round of voting on Commission membership, the Greek's language was rather tougher. For out of the five powers voted as candidates for the important Financial Commission, four – Peru, Brazil, Bolivia and Panama, in that order – came from Latin America. Perhaps understandably, Politis said it was 'shocking' that all the countries that had taken the 'most active' part in the war had been eliminated from the list, with the exception of Portugal. He might have added that two of those voted onto the Commission – Bolivia and Peru – had not even declared war. Latin American countries did almost equally well during voting for the Economic Commission. Brazil came top followed by China, Cuba, Siam (Thailand) and Ecuador; not a single European nation was on the list. [12]

The exasperated Greeks now persuaded the other European countries to abstain from voting on a supplementary 'reserve' list of countries that would be sent to the Supreme Council in case that body finally changed its mind and allowed more than five representatives. Ironically, Greece featured on both reserve lists, as did Belgium. But the damage was already done. What had started out as an apparently noble attempt by the smaller powers to make the Supreme Council sit up and take notice of them had descended into a rather less glorious squabble between the continents. Countries such as Belgium – which all agreed had suffered horribly in the war – had no one on either the Financial or Economic Commissions. Meanwhile, thanks to some continental solidarity – and backing from Siam and China – the main beneficiaries of this mini power-struggle appeared to be Panama, Cuba, Peru, Ecuador and Bolivia.

Latin American celebrations were short-lived, however. The members of the Supreme Council simply refused to allow two potentially important Commissions to have delegates from powers whose connection with the war was minimal and whose very presence at the Paris Peace Conference had been in doubt until the last minute. The Council therefore rejected the list of candidates and substituted their own. Out of deference to criticism about a lack of smaller state representation, the Great Powers did agree to increase the number of seats. However, they also completely changed the list of countries, substituting European nations for those that had originally been voted onto the Commissions. Only Brazil, an important ally of Washington and a country that had declared war, remained from the original list of Latin American countries. It was given a place on the Economic Commission. The feeling of satisfaction enjoyed by the delegates from Cuba, Panama, Ecuador, Bolivia and Peru at being voted onto the Commission now turned to anger. In their view there could be no greater evidence of the high-handedness of the Great Powers than this – being bounced off two Commissions they had been voted onto in accordance with Conference procedure.

Feelings were now running high among the Latin American states about the way they had been treated, especially Cuba and Panama, which had seen the prize of membership of key Commissions snatched away from them. Indeed, even before the Great Powers' decision, the Cuban delegation had been feeling aggrieved that it was not on the list of countries included on the Commission at the original vote on 3 March. Having arrived late for the Conference, Bustamante was now ill and recuperating at the city's Hotel Continental. So it fell to Rafael Martínez Ortíz and de Blanck to go and see Lansing's aide, Captain Van S Merle-Smith, on 4 March to complain about the way they had been treated. Their anger on this occasion, though, was not aimed at the Great Powers but at Brazil, which they believed had stitched them up.

Martínez Ortíz and de Blanck told the American that before the 3 March vote 'the Brazilian Delegates promised to the Cuban Representatives that they should have representation on one of the Committees', in other words either the Financial or the Economic Commission. 'However when the list was made up for presentation to the Five Powers, Brazil was included on both the Committees and Cuba was not represented on either,' they complained. 'Also, Brazil made no suggestion concerning the representation of Cuba.' The exchange shows the clear limitations of the so-called Latin American bloc, the implication being that Brazil had merely used the other states to further its own cause. Nor were the Cuban representatives themselves above advancing their own claims over those of other countries in the continent. For example, the diplomats pointed out that Uruguay, not having declared war, was 'not in a position equal to Cuba' while Panama 'had not the same basis of claim as the Cubans'. The Cubans believed that their status as a major sugar-exporting nation earned them the right to be on one of those key Commissions. While sympathetic, an American diplomat pointed out that Cuba already had a representative on the International Labour Organisation. Therefore 'I cannot see why she is entitled to representation on two committees, particularly in view of the fact that some of the other South American [sic] countries are not represented on any commissions'. [13]

After the Supreme Council's decision to throw all of the Latin American countries – bar Brazil – off the two Commissions it was the turn of other states to express their anger. Panama had already indicated at the start of the Conference that it was unhappy at the way it was being treated by the United States. Now it was getting similar treatment from both the United States and the other major Western Powers. On 13 March its delegation fired off a terse message to the Supreme Council of the Allies. This angry note pointed out that Panama had maintained 'as decided an attitude' towards Germany as Brazil and China 'who are appearing today as members of the Economic Commission and of other Commissions named previously'. Panama had suffered both 'morally and materially considerable damage in comparison to the extent of its territory and its modest economic situation' and yet was not included on 'any of the commissions thus far authorised by the Supreme Council of the Allies'. It concluded: 'The Delegation considers that its tacit acceptance of the resolution taken by the Supreme Council of the Allies to annul an election authorised by it and made freely and legitimately is indicative of the abandonment of a right which at least morally cannot be taken away.' [14]

Other Latin American states excluded from the Commissions felt equally angry. So furious were they that at a series of impromptu meetings held among them there was talk among some of them about walking out of the Paris Peace Conference. Indeed, their threats went further still. An American account of the meetings stated that 'some of the [Latin American delegates] have gone so far as to say they should ... possibly try to make a separate peace with Germany'. It was an astounding suggestion, and had it been carried out would have been a major propaganda setback for the Allies. Nor was that all. In a worried memo to President Wilson, Secretary of State Lansing and other members of the US delegation warned that Wilson's pet project of the League of Nations might also be at threat. 'There were also remarks made to the effect that if such an action as this on the part of the powerful nations was to be an indication of what the Great Powers would do in the League of Nations, it was best for them not to enter the League.' The Latin American delegates knew their audience; they were certainly very aware how much the League meant to Wilson and calculated that this threat alone would get his attention. After all, what message would it give about 'his' League if it started life being boycotted by nations from the United States' own backyard?[15]

Lansing's concern was apparent, as he wrote of the 'very hard feelings against the Great Powers', the 'insult' that the countries felt had been delivered to Latin America and the 'crisis' that had now occurred as a result. He was worried in particular that if the situation was not mollified, the 'feeling of resentment will undoubtedly react most unfavorably on the cause of the Associated Governments, and may give an opportunity for German propaganda, which is only dormant in South and Central America, to work on their feelings and impair the work which is being done at the Conference'. Moreover, as the United States was a member of the group of nations held responsible for decisions about Commission membership, it was coming in for its share of the 'resentment against the Great Powers'. Lansing cautioned that '… our relations with Latin America may be seriously impaired if we do not do all in our power to better the situation.'

However, Lansing also understood that the main issue of concern for countries such as Panama and Cuba was not the work of the Financial and Economic Commissions per se but 'pride'. Eventually, with the aid of some careful diplomacy, the American delegation helped soothe the simmering South and Central American indignation. The threat to quit the talks and negotiate with Germany had, after all, been a 'diplomatic threat' – one intended to make sure the other side (in this case the Great Powers) took notice of the complaint.[16]

The Commissions 'affair' had shown both the potential and the limitations of a Latin American 'bloc' working in concert at the Conference, and certainly shows that if there was also a smaller powers bloc then it was very limited in effect. Cuba's complaints, in particular, suggest that Brazil – the supposed leader of the Latin American grouping – was at times rather more interested in its own rewards than continental solidarity.

Another sign of a sense of resentment between the Latin states came in April. One of the Uruguayan delegation, Juan Carlos Blanco, sent the heads of the British, American, French and Italian delegations a letter in which he complained about his country not being invited to a recent meeting at the Ministry of Foreign Affairs in Paris. His country, he said, 'wishes to be able to follow, like the other nations taking part in the conference, the preliminaries of the peace with Germany'. Blanco said that information should be given to Uruguay 'at the same time as other nations invited to the Peace Conference'. What really seems to have hurt is that some of those 'other nations' which Blanco felt were getting information before Uruguay were countries who had 'not participated in any way' in the war. They had been invited simply because they had 'declared hostilities' against Germany. Though he does not mention any particular nation by name, it is clear Blanco is referring to the Central American and Caribbean countries.[17]

The complaint by smaller nations that they felt left out of much of the important business of Conference was a familiar theme of these six months. In one sense it was to be expected. For two of the Great Powers, Britain and especially France, the Conference was about how to create peace in Europe, and how both to punish Germany and ensure that France would never again have to face a devastating war with its neighbour. Countries such as Honduras, Haiti or Panama could expect to have little or no say in such matters. Yet having been invited to the gathering, it was also only natural for each country to want to particulate as fully a possible; and, like Uruguay, they felt aggrieved and patronised when kept in the dark or excluded from discussions. The smaller nations tended to be very sensitive to such slights, whether perceived or real. A good example of this came in May as one of the dramatic moments of the Conference approached: the handing of the peace terms to the defeated Germans.

Tension and excitement had been growing in the French capital for some days. On 28 April the German delegation selected for the dubious honour of receiving the Allies' peace terms had left Berlin for the Peace Conference. As they passed through the areas worst affected by the brutal conflict, the French authorities deliberately slowed down their train to ensure the visiting delegation got a good look. Then, once in Paris, it became something of a spectator sport to watch the German delegates as they came and went from their hotel. Meanwhile the day approached when the Germans, led by Ulrich Graf von Brockdorff-Rantzau, were to go to the Trianon Palace Hotel and learn what the terms were. The scheduled date was 7 May; and for all the delegates it was to be one of the most dramatic and historic moments of the gathering.

The Cuban delegation, however, felt not excitement but dismay as the day loomed closer, for they had been reading French press reports that some of the smaller nations, including Cuba, had not been invited to attend this historic event. It was for Cuba and other countries in the same position yet more proof that there were two Conferences taking place in Paris – one which really mattered and decided big issues for the most powerful countries, and another for everyone else. For various reasons – late arrival, then illness – Cuba's delegate Bustamante had not played as big a role at the Conference as he might have liked. Now, however, he sprang into action, firing off a letter to the President of the Conference, Clemenceau, though making sure he also sent a copy to Lansing. For all their differences with and objections to Washington policy in recent years, the Central American and Caribbean states knew that the United States was still their biggest ally at the Conference.

Writing in French, Bustamante pointedly told Clemenceau they had discovered *through the press* that the Republic of Cuba, which was the first Latin American state to declare war on Germany and which had made sacrifices and used up considerable resources for the Allied cause, had not been invited to be present at the handing over of the peace terms to the German representatives. He continued: *This must doubtless result from an oversight or from inaccurate information, given that representatives from the press will be present even though they have no official mission. Their presence there, however justified, should not prevent the presence of the belligerent powers.* Continuing his tone of restrained anguish, Bustamante concluded: *I would be very grateful if you would give the necessary instructions to correct this omission, which would be much appreciated by the nation that I have the honour to represent.* The letter was written the day before the peace terms were due to be handed to the Germans. Whether it was through Bustamante's intervention or for some other reason, all the Conference delegates were indeed present for the 7 May meeting. There, von Brockdorff-Rantzau's sometimes defiant speech caused great upset to the Allied leaders.[18]

The smaller nations had had absolutely no say in what the peace terms handed to the Germans contained; that remained firmly the responsibility of Wilson, Clemenceau, Lloyd George, Italy's Vittorio Orlando and their teams. This did not, however, stop the eloquent Policarpo Bonilla from trying to influence one key point: the fate of the German wartime leader Kaiser Wilhelm II. This issue had been a major source of contention between the Great Powers, and especially between the United States, Britain and France. The Europeans wanted the Kaiser, who had fled to Holland, to be put on trial for war crimes. President Wilson was less sure and his Secretary of State was quite opposed, believing there was no international legal basis for such a move. Eventually, however, the American delegation reluctantly agreed to accept articles in the Treaty calling for the Dutch to extradite the Kaiser so that he could face a charge of what was called 'a supreme offence against international morality …'.

Given the Americans' deep misgivings over seeking to put the Kaiser on trial, they may have been privately pleased when Bonilla expressed his own misgivings in a note read out at the Plenary Conference the day before the terms of peace were to be given to the vanquished. Bonilla, who had trained as a lawyer, said that it was an *uncontested principle of natural law that no man may be tried or punished except for an offence already and explicitly defined and made punishable by law.* He continued: *The Delegation of [Honduras] considers that there is no case for the trial of William II of Hohenzollern, ex-German Emperor ... there is indeed no international law or precedent for trying him. The head of a State is only responsible to his own people; his people can neither try nor condemn him except in accordance with regularly established laws. In the present case it would be more logical to try and condemn the whole German people, which tolerated and abetted the acts of its governors ... .* As with Bonilla's interjection over the Monroe Doctrine in the League Covenant, there was not the remotest chance that the former Honduran President's arguments would influence the outcome, even if in this case Lansing and other Americans may have agreed with him.[19]

The Peace Conference was now approaching its climactic moment, the signing of the Treaty of Versailles. On this occasion there would be no question of the smaller nations not attending as their delegates all had to sign the Treaty, even if much of it had been agreed with no input from them. The event took place on 28 June and the spectacular venue chosen for it was the Hall of Mirrors at the Palace of Versailles. The Central American and Caribbean delegates, Guilbaud, Méndez, Chamorro, Bustamante, Bonilla and Burgos filed in with the other representatives to take their seats in the spectacular setting. Theirs was literally a walk on, walk off role. Once Clemenceau had opened the proceedings, all eyes were on the two German delegates as they came forward and signed the Treaty. Then it was the turn of the delegates from the victorious states to add their signature to the Treaty. By the time the last of them had signed, the other representatives were standing around chatting while the Bolivian delegate nervelessly asked the German pair for their autographs. Finally it was all over. A terrible war had been concluded with a monumental peace. That night there were celebrations held by relieved delegations throughout Paris. Just how much the Central American and Caribbean delegates would have to cheer at the outcome of the Treaty was unclear. For them the big achievement of this document was the establishment of the League of Nations, potentially a bulwark against American intervention in the region. But within the coming months, that bulwark was to be weakened.

Senor Don Joaquin Mendez from Guatemala and Senor Don Diego Manuel Chamorro from Nicaragua in 1920.

The Legacy

6

Honduras and Guatemala

In common with the other Central American and Caribbean participants in Paris, Guatemala and Honduras quickly ratified the Treaty of Versailles, enabling them to become founding members of the League of Nations. This was one tangible achievement for these countries from a Conference at which their presence had, for the most part, and especially in the case of Guatemala, been inconspicuous to the point of irrelevance. Here was a chance for a permanent seat at the top table of world politics, in a body moreover whose membership had a very strong Latin American flavour. Though Ecuador inexplicably declined to ratify the Treaty and thus did not become a member of the League when it came into force in January 1920, all the other Latin American states that attended the Paris talks did so. To this were added some of the Latin American major powers which had stayed resolutely neutral in the war, such as Argentina and Chile.

Thus from the viewpoint of Tegucigalpa and Guatemala City there was every reason for cautious optimism that the new League would make a real difference to the future, notably in relation to the threat of intervention by Washington. The

League of Nations was an opportunity to be a member of the same club as the United States, a club in which all the members would have to abide by its rules. Under such an organisation, the territorial integrity of countries such as Honduras and Guatemala would not just be protected from attack by their immediate neighbours, but from American marines as well.

Their big concern, of course, was still the application of the Monroe Doctrine. They were dismayed that Article 21 of the League Covenant explicitly ruled out any conflict between it and the Doctrine. They were equally unhappy, as Policarpo Bonilla had made clear in Paris, that the Doctrine had remained undefined. For the countries of Latin America there was a real fear that this could water down the effectiveness of the League in its – to them – prime role of protecting them against Washington.

In the end, the power of the League in Latin American eyes was not just watered down but holed below the waterline by the failure of the United States to join the organisation. The fact that the United States did not become a founder member of the League of Nations probably came as little surprise to most observers, even though President Wilson had been its main champion. The strength of opposition from many Republicans in Washington had been apparent during the Peace Conference. Much of that opposition

MEXICO, PARIS AND THE LEAGUE
Mexico remained neutral during the First World War – indeed the Allies felt it favoured Germany – so there was never any real likelihood it would be invited to take part in the Paris Peace Conference. There was, however, still the question of whether Mexico should be invited to join the League of Nations, as were other neutral Latin American countries such as Argentina, Chile and El Salvador. Mexico was and remains a major power in the region. With the United States strongly against its admittance, Mexico was not invited to join, causing considerable anger there, even though it is by no means certain that it would have accepted membership under President Venustiano Carranza had it been offered.

was to the terms of Article 10, under which League members undertook to 'respect and preserve' against external aggression the 'territorial integrity and existing political independence' of all members. For Wilson this Article lay at the heart of the organisation's purpose, but for his opponents it undermined the role of Congress and ultimately the United States Constitution. An exhausting tour of the country by the ailing Wilson in September 1919 failed to overcome this determined opposition, and contributed to the President's worsening health. Congress refused to ratify the Treaty and membership of the League and later, in 1920, Republican Warren G Harding was voted into the White House. This virtually guaranteed that Washington would stay out of the League.

But if the absence of the Americans was no shock, it was still a major blow to those in South and Central America and the Caribbean. They had pinned their hopes on the troublesome Article 10, the very Article that had aroused such opposition in Washington. Those hopes were now dashed. America's decision had two implications for Latin America. First, Washington retained the same freedom to act as it had always done in the region. Secondly, there was the reaction of the League to Washington's absence.

The League's first General Assembly held in November 1920 was not greeted with much enthusiasm around the world. One British newspaper said that while in 1919 the start of the organisation's work had been eagerly awaited as an historic event of 'profound significance', it was now little more than a 'sorry farce'.[1] Reaction was little better in other key countries such as France and Italy. General Secretary Sir Eric Drummond was even worried that Britain might follow America's lead and quit the League. The organisation thus played a delicate balancing act. On the one hand it had to reflect the views of its members, more than a quarter of who were from Latin America. Yet equally it had no wish to antagonise the United States, whose tacit support for much of the League's work would be important in the coming years. As a result, the League trod very carefully on issues affecting the United States' 'backyard' of Central America and the Caribbean. Without the membership of Washington, the League's level of realistic protection for Central American and Caribbean states was little more than a fig leaf.[2]

In these circumstances it is perhaps unsurprising that some Latin American members of the League quickly grew disillusioned. In 1921 Argentina withdrew after a squabble over who should be members of the organisation and how members of the ruling Council should be chosen. Buenos Aires did not resume full membership until 1933. In 1926 Brazil, which had been one of the non-permanent members of the Council, and saw itself as the voice of Latin America in Geneva, quit after its demand to be a permanent council member was rejected. Meanwhile the demeanour of some Latin American delegates irritated other League members, partly through their tendency to hold up pan-American cooperation as a model for the way the League should behave.

Honduras can hardly be said to have played a prominent role in League issues. Indeed for the first three Assemblies in Geneva, there is no record of an Honduran delegate having participated. It was not until the fourth Assembly in September 1923 that Carlos Gutierrez, the Chargé d'Affaires in Paris, attended as the Honduran representative. He also took the opportunity to sign the International Convention for the Suppression of the Circulation of and Traffic in Obscene Publications on behalf of his country. Even this appearance was a rarity; the next League of Nations Assembly to record the presence of a Honduran delegate was the tenth one in 1929. On this occasion the representative was Froylan Turcios, a former Minister of the Interior, diplomat, writer and leading Honduran intellectual noted for his bitter opposition to United States intervention in Central America. The country's somewhat tenuous relationship with the organisation formally ended when on 10 July 1936 it gave notice that it was quitting, one of a number of Latin American countries who had by then found the League to be utterly irrelevant.

Honduras' delegate at Paris Policarpo Bonilla had been busy after the Conference ended. For a brief period in mid-1919 he had become captivated by the idea of increasing links between Honduras and France, possibly as a way of lessening American influence in his country. His idea included sending Hondurans to train in French military academies, allowing French officers to reform the Honduran police force, setting up a regular shipping service between the two nations, and increasing banking and economic ties. The French government was sufficiently keen on the idea to appoint the officer who would reform the Honduran police. But by then Bonilla had left on an 'urgent' mission to Washington and none of the ideas were followed through. This was probably because the Honduran now had another more pressing project in mind, one that had preoccupied him for three decades.[3]

On 19 January 1921 representatives from four countries, Honduras, Guatemala, El Salvador and Costa Rica, met in San José to sign a Covenant of Union of Central America. This was the centenary year of the independence of the isthmian states. The document stated that the countries considered it 'their sacred and patriotic duty to complete as far as possible the reconstruction of the Federal Republic of Central America ...'. Unfortunately this new incarnation of the Federation lacked one key member: Nicaragua (Panama had not been part of the old United Provinces of Central America). 'The Contracting States sincerely regret that the sister Republic of Nicaragua does not immediately join,' read the covenant, while making it clear that it would still be welcome in the future. The agreement established the new Federation's legislative body, a National Constituent Assembly, among whose tasks it was to draw up a new constitution for the Federation. This body met in Tegucigalpa on 20 July 1921 amid much fanfare, with military salutes and celebrations. Its President was named as Policarpo Bonilla, that long-time champion of regional unity.[4]

It was a proud moment for Bonilla; apart from his time as President of Honduras, it was perhaps the pinnacle of his career. But it was to be short-lived. That same year a change of government in Guatemala saw that country pull out of the Federation, and the whole venture collapsed like a house of cards amid yet more inter-regional squabbling. For Bonilla it was his last real chance to see a unified Central America, and it had vanished almost as soon as it had materialised.

In 1923 the veteran politician had one more unsuccessful attempt at becoming President of Honduras but came second in a three-candidate race. At this point the outgoing President López Gutiérrez declared himself dictator and a civil war broke out. In March of that year the United States despatched marines to Tegucigalpa to restore order and broker a peace deal. The marines soon left but so did Bonilla, fleeing to self-imposed exile in San Salvador in 1924. After a year Bonilla left to travel to New Orleans, the scene of much of his plotting and scheming in previous years. His stay there did not last long. On 11 September 1926 Bonilla died there at the age of 68, the end of one of Honduras' more colourful political careers.

The 1923 election in which Bonilla had unsuccessfully fought saw the emergence of a figure that was to dominate Honduran politics for the next two decades. Tiburcio Carías Andino was the driving force behind the new National Party, which became the main opposition to the Liberals in the country. It was Carías' choice, Miguel Paz Barahona, who was elected as President in 1924 after the brief American intervention, and he ruled until 1929. After a three-year period in which the Liberals regained power, Carías himself was elected President in 1932. He then ruled as dictator until 1948, a period in Honduran politics referred to as the *Cariato*.

This was an era in Honduras when the banana industry dominated. By the end of the 1920s the trade in bananas accounted for close to 90 percent of the country's exports. The influence the trade had on Honduran politics only increased in 1929 when the larger UFCO bought out the Cuyamel Fruit Company, leaving Standard Fruit the only other main player in the country.

It was not all bad news economically. Honduras' long-running foreign debt problem had been largely resolved thanks to a deal agreed by the US Congress in 1926 to reschedule payments over a thirty-year period. This debt had been a millstone around the neck of successive regimes following a failed attempt to build an ocean-to-ocean railway in the 1870s with foreign loans. However, the country's utter dependence on one export product made Honduras exceptionally vulnerable to downturns in world trade, which is what happened in the 1930s with the onset of the Depression.

When Carías became President in February 1933 he inherited a troubled country. On top of a fall in tax revenue caused by a fall in banana prices in the early 1930s, compounded by disease hitting the crops after 1936, Liberal politicians had staged an armed rebellion in November of the previous year, further sapping the country's finances and energy. Ironically, given Carías' emergence as a dictator in subsequent years, he had since 1923 sought to establish a level of political stability in the country through the acceptance of both victories and defeats at the ballot box. His response to the current crisis, however, was typical of the tactics used by dictators emerging in other Central American nations in this period; even if Carías' rule is generally considered to be less harsh than those of some of his counterparts. He reduced the powers of the Honduran Congress to criticise government, established more centralized control over local authorities and clamped down on political opponents. One eye-catching symbol of his authoritarian role was the policy of using prisoners with iron balls chained to their legs to help construct buildings in Tegucigalpa.

Carías' legacy was one of limited achievements. His greatest was to bring to Honduran politics a relative order that was without precedent in recent decades – indeed, his period as dictator was the longest period without civil war since its independence. Under his rule Honduras also maintained its financial obligations, meeting foreign debt repayments even during the Depression when other countries defaulted. There were other achievements too, such as an improvement in the education system, a determined policy of road building in a nation hampered by poor communications, modernisation of the army – an institution that would play an increasingly key role in Honduran politics – and attempts to diversify the economy away from its dependence on bananas and mining, notably towards a development of the coffee industry.

Yet Honduras remained a desperately poor country. Indeed in 1942 it was officially the poorest republic not just in Central

America but in the whole of Latin America. It had few inhabitants and they were thinly scattered across its lands: a census in 1930 recorded just 854,148 people, which meant the population density was lower than 20 people per square mile. In population terms the capital, Tegucigalpa, was just a small town, with a mere 40,000 inhabitants. As elsewhere in Central America, the post-First World War period had seen the emergence of the middle and working classes. Even though neither was yet a major political force there was a growing demand for social reform and workers' rights inspired not just by the Russian Revolution of 1917 but also by one closer to home – in Mexico. Fear of organised labour movements led Carías to suppress workers' demonstrations to the benefit, of course, of the banana multinationals. The dictator's control of the country's political institutions and his suppression of opposition politics also further undermined democracy in a nation where it was already frail. The country still suffered from a chronic lack of efficient administration and financial economic planning.

Honduras' policy approach to the Second World War was broadly similar to that which it had pursued in the First World War. Though a dictator, Carías seems not to have had much sympathy for either Adolf Hitler or Benito Mussolini – unlike some of his regional counterparts. His regime followed the United States' neutrality at the outbreak of the conflict, and then declared war on Japan on 8 December 1941 shortly after the attack on Pearl Harbor, and on Germany on 13 December. While some other Central American states joined the Allied side purely out of cynical self-interest, it appears that Carías was at least partly motivated by a genuine willingness to show continental solidarity with the United States.

Carías, partly through his own design, partly perhaps

through pressure from the United States, chose not to stand when presidential elections were held in 1948. Instead his handpicked successor was Juan Manuel Gálvez, a former lawyer for UFCO. Nonetheless the new President showed both a surprising independence of mind from his political mentor and a willingness to promote reforms. For the first time the fruit multinationals had to pay income tax and there were also efforts to modernise the economy, build more roads, power plants and telecommunications, and reform the banking system. His Presidency also experienced a major strike by banana plantation workers in 1954 that won them higher wages and trade union recognition. In the presidential elections of the same year Carías failed in his bid to regain the Presidency, a result he accepted without recourse to violence.

However Julio Lozano Díaz, who had become temporary President after Gálvez retired on health grounds, stayed in office as dictator. The military, a more professional body now than it had been in the past, deposed Lozano on the grounds that his rule was unconstitutional. It then held good to its promise to hold fresh elections, which were won in 1957 by the Liberal Ramón Villeda Morales. He ruled until 1963, extending many of the reforms carried out by his immediate predecessors. It looked as if Honduras was embarking on a period of relative political calm, before the army intervened in 1963, establishing military rule for the next two decades.

Like Honduras, Guatemala had ratified the Treaty of Versailles and became a founder member of the League of Nations. It sent no fewer than three delegates to the first meeting of the General Assembly in Geneva on 15 November 1920: Manuel Valladares y Aycinerra, Manuel Arroyo and Julio Herrera. However, in common with other countries in the region, Guatemala's enthusiasm for the organisation waned, partly because of the absence of the United States from its ranks and thus the League's general irrelevance to events in the isthmus. It announced its decision to quit the organisation in May 1936. As with Honduras, the last remaining legacy of the Paris Peace Conference had withered away.

The League's General Secretary Sir Eric Drummond believed that the lack of enthusiasm shown by countries such as Guatemala was partly a result of manoeuvring by Washington. 'In spite of the assurances given by officials and others in the United States that they have no hostility to the League, it is certain that private or even semi-official action of the United States is directed against new application for entry into the League, against the countries of South and Central America taking much interest in the League, and if a country in that Continent leaves the League (an event which causes them no sorrow) against its return,' he said.[5]

By the time Guatemala's delegates took up their seats at the first League General Assembly, the quixotic and despotic ruler who had ruled the country for twenty-two years had finally gone. Manuel Estrada Cabrera had managed to maintain a fine balancing act between supporting the United States' interests and those of its major fruit companies, and a level of diplomatic independence. His policies had up until 1919 won the grudging respect, if not the love, of Washington. By early 1920, however, President Woodrow Wilson had reached the conclusion that the increasingly bizarre regime of Estrada Cabrera, a frequent meddler in the affairs of his country's neighbours, was no longer the best guarantor of United States interest in that country or the region as whole. The knowledge in late 1919 and early 1920 that Washington would not oppose Estrada Cabrera's overthrow gave renewed energy to internal opposition, and in April 1920 the National

Assembly ruled that he was mentally unfit to govern. After a brief outbreak of violence Estrada Cabrera surrendered. He was later tried and jailed but released on health grounds. He died in 1924.

Cabrera's overthrow led to Guatemala's brief flirtation with a unified Central America, but a change of regime led to its rapid demise, and thereafter government fell into the hands of two generals, first José María Orellana and then Lázaro Chacón, who was in power until 1930. In Guatemala, as elsewhere in the region, the 1920s saw a rise in attempts by workers to organise themselves as a significant social force. The country's rulers were not entirely deaf to the calls for more rights and better conditions. The International Labour Organisation (ILO) – on whose Commission Cuba's delegate in Paris, Bustamante, had sat – established minimum standards for workers in 1919 and through the League of Nations the ILO sought to apply them worldwide. Guatemala signed up to those standards in 1926. Yet it is hard to say that the lot of the average worker in Guatemala in this decade improved significantly.

There were a number of factors that made Guatemala slightly different from its neighbours. One was that of a larger population than other countries in the isthmus, recorded at 1.7 million in 1930. Another was the proximity of Mexico, a powerful neighbour that Guatemalan rulers had always feared, a feeling only strengthened by the Mexican Revolution and its wide-ranging attempts at social reform. Such developments alarmed the elite class of white and *ladino* landowners who still wielded enormous power in Guatemala, a class-conscious country where around 70 percent of the population was Indian. This meant there was little appetite for social reform among most of the ruling classes. Coupled with a desire on behalf of successive rulers to ensure that UFCO prospered, this social conservatism ensured that the country's rulers were usually supported in their quest for stability and order in preference to reform and progress. When unrest broke out in parts of neighbouring El Salvador in early 1932, the fears of Guatemala's landowners and elites only grew.

It was into this climate of apprehension at the start of the Depression years – when the country's economic mainstay industry coffee was badly hit by a fall in prices – that the former War Minister General Jorge Ubico emerged as the country's dictator. Ubico was elected President in February 1931 and ruled the country as dictator for thirteen years. This was an era of dictatorships in the region, for example in Honduras and Nicaragua; the trend can be seen as the ruling classes in Central America attempting to control the newly emerging working and middle classes through strong government. In Guatemala's case, there was also plenty of precedent. The country had a history of *caudillo* rulers or strongman dictators and Ubico was very much in the same mould as men such as Estrada Cabrera. Ubico even shared his predecessor's tendency towards eccentricity, enjoying, for example, dispensing his views to his people via the press and airwaves on music, mechanics and cooking. He was also a great admirer of Napoleon Bonaparte – he appears to have believed he was a reincarnation of the Frenchman – and loved riding around the country on a motorbike. There was, however, little of charm about much of Ubico's methods. He emasculated the country's Congress, built up a secret police force, disbanded trade unions and tolerated no opposition and free discussion of ideas. Anyone committing a crime against a foreigner was quickly and harshly punished. In 1932 Ubico launched a brutal suppression of communists in the country, effectively destroying Guatemala's Communist Party.

Ubico's success in staying in power was largely due to his ability to balance competing interests much as Cabrera had done. He continued the traditional support for UFCO – and by extension the United States – and also generally backed the country's coffee plantation owners. At the same time he abolished debt slavery among the country's peasants, a move that reduced the hold of plantation owners over rural workers. Ubico used a mixture of populism and paternalism to court the support of the rural masses. Combined with his ruthless suppression of dissident voices though his secret police force, Ubico's cynical juggling act with different sectors of society proved effective. As he is once said to have remarked, 'I have no friends, only domesticated enemies.'[6]

Despite Germany's defeat in the First World War, German influence in the country was still significant, especially in the coffee industry. German planters, many of them based in the Alta Verapaz region, produced as much as half of the country's entire coffee output. Ubico was also an admirer of Adolf Hitler. Yet when the Second World War broke out, Ubico's first concern, as always, was pragmatic self-interest. He moved swiftly to deport certain German nationals at the start of the war and later nationalised their coffee estates. When the United States was attacked at Pearl Harbor, Guatemala

COSTA RICA AND EL SALVADOR
Costa Rica emerged as the most stable and socially progressive of the Central American republics. The country adopted a measure of welfare reforms early in the 20th century – not unlike Uruguay – and with a few exceptions a relatively stable party political system developed. The exceptions were the short-lived Tinoco regime which coincided with the 1919 Paris Peace Conference and a brief but bloody civil war in 1948. By contrast El Salvador, having enjoyed relative stability in the early decades of the 20th century, witnessed a bloody peasant rebellion in 1932 that left thousands dead. The country was then governed by authoritarian military and conservative civilian rulers for many decades to come.

was quick to declare war on Japan, Italy and Germany, and welcomed the stationing of American troops on its soil. It was a form of 'geographical fatalism'; no matter what his personal views of the Nazi regime in Germany, the United States would always be the near neighbour of Guatemala and thus key to its economic well-being.

Though the coffee trade with the United States helped keep Guatemala's economy afloat during the war, Ubico was coming under increasing pressure domestically. The impact of inflation and the exposure of the country's middle classes and students to democratic views espoused by the country's wartime allies led to growing discontent with the inward-looking and shuttered regime. 'While I am President I will not grant liberty of the press nor of association because the people of Guatemala are not prepared for democracy and need a firm hand,' he declared defiantly in June 1944 following student protests. But faced with increasing protests Ubico quickly realised his time in charge was over and quit. Soon afterwards, on 20 October 1944, a group of young army officers enlisted popular support to stage a revolt.[7]

Thirteen months earlier, on 28 September 1943, Joaquin Méndez had died at the age of 82 in Guatemala City. After his time in Paris at the Peace Conference, Méndez had continued his career as a diplomat in the United States, where, apart from his time in Paris, he lived for 27 years from 1911. As well as being a diplomat, Mendez had also been a correspondent for the press across Latin America from the United States. He and his American wife Elizabeth Kramer, who survived him, had three sons and two daughters. Mendez had played a low-key role at the Peace Conference, his brief being essentially to support United States policy on behalf of his country. Much of his time in government service had been under dictators; first Estrada Cabrera, then Ubico. He did not live long enough to see the changes occur in his country.

After Ubico's downfall and the October revolt, Guatemala staged free elections in 1945. The result was a decade of reform in the country that saw workers' and peasants' rights enshrined, workers' pay increased, the education system reformed, and civil and political liberties bestowed. The two Presidents who oversaw this significant, though far from revolutionary programme, were first Juan José Arévalo and then Jacobo Arbenz. Both partially modelled their reforms on the Mexican model so feared by Ubico and many of the country's landowners.

Their biggest area of change was in land reform. This began in earnest in 1952, when 1.5 million acres began to be redistributed to 100,000 new owners. Some of the land earmarked for expropriation was owned by UFCO. This set off alarm bells in Washington, where many senior figures had close ties to the fruit giant. The United States, now in the grip of the Cold War, had already become nervous about an Arbenz regime that many felt was too accommodating to Communism.

By the middle of 1953 American diplomats had started an offensive against Guatemala, branding its regime as a threat to regional security. This was the era of the 'domino theory', the argument that if one country in the region fell to Communism or Soviet influence, the rest could likewise succumb. Aware that it faced possible removal by force, the Arbenz government meanwhile ordered weapons from Eastern Europe. Then the Central Intelligence Agency took a key role in events, supporting an invasion by a group of armed insurgents in 1954 led by a Guatemalan colonel Carlos Castillo Armas from across the border in Honduras. The Guatemalan army, which up to then had largely stayed out of events, first fought the invaders then stopped its resistance. This, and (unfounded) fears of a bigger invasion force persuaded Arbenz to step down, and Castillo Armas was soon installed as President.

Guatemala's experiment with social reform was over. The clock was soon turned back, and even after Castillo Armas's assassination in 1957 the conservatism of the counter-revolution continued under General Manuel Ydígoras Fuentes, who had once been Ubico's Minister of Public Works. Guatemala's politics had become fatally polarised between left and right, with little middle ground remaining.

7

Panama and Nicaragua

Given the strong backing given to the League of Nations by Antonio Burgos during the Paris Peace Conference, it was only to be expected that Panama would quickly ratify the Treaty of Versailles and became a founding member of the organisation. It sent two delegates to the first General Assembly in Geneva in 1920. Their prominence suggests the importance that the country attached to the League at this time. Harmodio Arias was a smart lawyer from an upwardly mobile landowning family and would later be President of Panama, while Narciso Garay would soon serve as his country's Foreign Minister. However, the failure of the United States to become part of the organisation was a bitter blow for Panama. President Belisario Porras had made it clear to Burgos in Paris that the country was irritated by the way it was being treated by Washington and was anxious to find means to persuade the United States to change its stance. The League had promised such an opportunity.

The lack of 'consideration' with which President Porras felt the United States treated his country was demonstrated by a boundary dispute with Costa Rica, which at one point in

1921 threatened to break out into war between the two neighbours. The origins of the dispute over the Coto region went back many years, to when Panama was part of Colombia. In 1910 both countries had agreed to a suggestion by the United States that the matter be arbitrated by Chief Justice Edward Douglass White Jr of the Supreme Court of the United States. Yet when the verdict fell, Panama rejected it on the grounds that the judge had exceeded his remit in reaching his decision. In early 1921 Costa Rica, impatient with the lack of progress in the matter, sent a small force to occupy the disputed Coto region. Panamanian forces repelled over the mini 'invasion', and the United States, alarmed at a possible war so close to the Panama Canal, felt obliged to step in. Secretary of State Charles Hughes justified his diplomatic intervention by invoking Article I of the 1903 Hay Bunau-Varilla Treaty between Panama and the United States, under which the latter had the right to guarantee the independence of Panama. In American eyes this meant the ability to ascertain for itself the proper boundaries of Panama. The United States urged Panama to accept the 1914 White ruling and called for it to remove its troops from the disputed region. In effect Washington was reserving the right to dictate Panama's foreign policy in order to guarantee its independence.

President Porras was furious. The previous autumn he had met the then President-Elect of the United States Warren G Harding when the latter had taken a holiday in Panama. The two men had got on well, with Harding apparently promising to ensure that the two nations had 'the most friendly relations'.[1] Now Porras tried to use this understanding by appealing directly to President Harding over the head of his Secretary of State. In a telegram to the White House, Porras said that the demand from the State Department for Panama to accept the White ruling was 'painful and humiliating', especially as the arbitrator had exceeded his powers and given Costa Rica 'more than what her representative ... asked'. He continued, 'I appeal, therefore, directly to you Mr President, recalling your kind words with which you expressed your friendship and good wishes towards my country when you honored us with your visit in November.' He begged the American President to use his influence to ensure that the boundary dispute 'may have a solution more in accord with justice and dignity than the one we are being asked to accept'. Other Panamanian politicians also pointed out that Panama 'is not allowed by the United States to have arms', so the only weapons her men had used were 'the guns which her men had captured from Costa Rica'.[2] Unfortunately for Porras and Panama, President Harding backed his Secretary of State's call and despite further protestations, an angry Panama government felt obliged to withdraw its troops on 23 August.

Panamanian frustration at the United States was part of the reason that the country backed a novel solution to both the current dispute and Latin American disputes in general – and that was the creation of a Pan-American League of Nations similar to the one created at Paris for the whole world. The idea was put forward by Cuba's former delegate in Paris and international law expert Antonio Sánchez de Bustamante. He tabled a number of suggestions for solving the dispute between Costa Rica and Panama, while backing the latter's refusal to accept the White arbitration on the issue.

Among the ideas put forward by Bustamante was an agreement between the two countries under which *the inhabitants of the disputed territories are called upon to decide their own destinies*. Another proposal was to make an *appeal to the League of Nations within the terms of the Treaty of*

Versailles. However it was another proposal that was most intriguing. Bustamante suggested: *A Pan-American agreement of good offices, of mediation or of arbitration that would inaugurate the League of American Nations for controversies and doctrines of this part of the world.* Crucially, and doubtless aimed at an American audience, Bustamante added: *Such a league would not conflict with the Monroe Doctrine.*[3]

The idea for an American League received strong backing from Panama's Foreign Minister Narcisco Garay who, having already been his country's delegate to the first General Assembly of the League of Nations, had first-hand knowledge of how such a body could operate. 'Such a league would be more than agreeable to the nations of North, South and Central America, particularly those that have joined the League provided by the Treaty of Versailles,' said the Foreign Minister. Narcisco Garay made clear the dissatisfaction of many Latin America countries at being a member of a League of Nations that had no formal influence over the United States, while hinting that the cost of sending delegates to Geneva and supporting the League was also an issue for his country. 'Under existing conditions these nations [i.e. Latin American members of the League] are paying their share of the expense of the League, but unless the United States should join the League, the American nations reap none of its benefits because of the workings of the Monroe Doctrine.'[4]

The idea of a League of American Nations made no initial progress, but the following year it was picked up by another former delegate to the Paris Peace Conference, Uruguay's Juan Antonio Buero. He and Uruguayan President Baltasar Brum said such a league should be based on the 'absolute equality of all of them', and among other advantages it would

enable nations to coordinate their views ahead of world meetings. 'If as we wish the League is formed ... the Americas will
become ever stronger and more closely united in the League,'
said Buero.[5] The Panamanian/ Uruguayan/ Cuban idea was
then raised at the Fifth International Conference of American
States held in Santiago in 1923. It provoked sufficient interest to be sent to the Governing Board of the Pan-American
Union for more detailed consideration, but nothing came of
it. However the Santiago gathering did agree a mechanism to
resolve disputes between member countries.

Meanwhile tensions remained between Panama and the
United States, their destinies doomed to be entwined by their
common interest in the Panama Canal Zone. The Panama-
nians continued to press for a change in the 1903 Treaty,
objecting not just to the Americans' self-proclaimed right
to guarantee Panama's independence but also over the exact
status of the Canal Zone itself. The Americans insisted the
Treaty meant it had full sovereignty over the narrow strip of
land, while Panama considered it shared sovereignty there.
As early as 1904 the Taft Agreement had been signed to help
resolve the Canal Zone issue, but with only partial success. In
1926 a new treaty designed to replace the Taft Agreement was
signed, but rejected by Panama's National Assembly the following year. The Assembly members believed the new Treaty
was little more than a reiteration of the 1904 Agreement,
with the unwelcome addition of a clause that would oblige
Panama to join the United States in any war.

The 1903 Treaty and the Taft Agreement thus remained
in force, a lingering source of discontent on the Panamanian
side. Significant change only occurred in the 1930s with an
evolution in US foreign policy toward the region. As early as
the 1920s Washington had begun to adjust its approach to

the Caribbean and Central America, reducing its emphasis on direct and armed intervention and putting more weight on regional cooperation, even if this change in policy was not always evident from a Central American perspective. It culminated in the so-called Good Neighbor Policy announced by President Franklin D Roosevelt in his inaugural address in 1933. Later that year at the Seventh International Conference of American States in Montevideo Roosevelt's Secretary of State Cordell Hull signed up to a convention which contained the article: 'No state has the right to intervene in the internal or external affairs of another.' This helped convince Latin American nations, including Panama, that Washington's policy was moving in the right direction. But not entirely. For Hull had reserved the US's right to act 'by the laws of nations as generally recognised', a qualification which dismayed Latin American nations.[6]

By 1936 Panama had already achieved a measure of satisfaction over its claims from the Roosevelt Administration. In 1933 President Harmodio Arias – the former delegate to the League of Nations – met with Roosevelt in Washington, and the two governments agreed Panama should control all commercial rights within the Canal Zone, with Washington also accepting there should not be any American business there which was harmful to Panamanian interests. This went some way to satisfying Panamanian concerns over the day-to-day operation of the Canal Zone. Then in March 1936, after two years of negotiations, the two countries signed a General Treaty of Friendship and Cooperation under which the United States agreed to lose the right to guarantee Panama's independence and its right to intervene in the country and expropriate additional land or sea territory in order to support and protect the Canal. The money paid to Panama by the United States under the 1903 Treaty – which was amended rather than appealed by the new Agreement – was also increased to $430,000 a year.

The 1936 Treaty thus went some way to meeting Panamanian complaints, though not entirely. On the American side there were doubts too. The United States Congress only approved ratification of the new Agreement in 1939 after an exchange of diplomatic letters between the two countries made it clear that while Washington had a duty to consult with Panama over any military action, it could act first and consult later.

By this time Panama had grown ever more disenchanted with the League of Nations, at which it was represented for five years by its Paris delegate Antonio Burgos. Panama's frustration with the League was of course partly due to the expense, partly because of the United States' continuing and now clearly permanent absence from that body. But there was also dissatisfaction with the way that the League handled other issues far from the Americas but which showed – in Panamanian eyes – a worrying lack of support for countries under attack. So, for example, when after the Japanese invasion of Manchuria in 1931 the League's response was to set up a commission to 'study and report' on the issue, the reaction in Panama was one of dismay and apprehension. If the League could react so timidly to protect Manchuria, what would it be able to do to help a tiny nation such as Panama? Nonetheless, unlike its Central American neighbours, Panama did not withdraw from the League, and stayed on as a member until the organisation's demise.[7] League membership, the last vestige of its participation at the Paris Peace Conference, was something it was reluctant to relinquish.

Domestically, the 1930s proved equally eventful for Panama.

In 1931 Arnulfo Arias Madrid had led a palace coup that saw Florencio Arosemena deposed as President – Arias reportedly held a gun to his head – and resulted in his older brother Harmodio becoming temporary President. He then won the presidential election the following year. The younger brother remained a key influence, and as Ambassador to Italy in this period he also whetted his enthusiasm for Mussolini's fascist regime. Arnulfo Arias also visited Germany under Hitler.

Another representative to Italy in the 1930s had been Peace Conference delegate Antonio Burgos, who after spells in Spain and Cuba had been Panama's Minister in Rome. On 2 August 1937 Burgos died in Italy from a cerebral haemorrhage at the age of 64 after a lifetime of public and diplomatic service to his country. In addition to his diplomatic career, Burgos had been a prodigious author, penning books on a wide array of subjects including commercial monopolies and an ambitious political geography of the world. During his career abroad the Panamanian had also picked up an impressive collection of awards from foreign countries, including Spain, Portugal, Italy, Romania, Serbia and Montenegro. Burgos was also a link with Panama's past, having been one of those who had signed the original constitution of this new country.

Back in Panama, the younger Arias became President in 1940 at a critical time for the world in general and the Panama Canal in particular. Once in power, Arias adopted policies that seemed inspired by his interest in fascism: there were laws discriminating against Afro-Caribbean and Asian Pana-manians, restrictions on foreigners and attempts to run the economy on centralised lines. Washington viewed events in the country with increasing concern. A regime with totalitar-ian tendencies was bad enough. But under Arias the country was also dragging its heels on negotiations to install new

American bases that the military felt necessary to protect the canal in case the war in Europe became a worldwide conflict. In such an eventuality this narrow stretch of water connecting the Pacific and Atlantic Oceans would become one of the most strategically vital spots on the planet. There were meanwhile rumours – never substantiated – that Arias' family were providing provisions to German submarine crews from one of their farms on the Caribbean coast. Arias' sympathies for the fascist regimes in Europe were certainly seen by Washington as a potential threat to regional security.

In October 1941, while he was out of the country, Arias was deposed by a coup carried out with the backing or at least the knowledge of the United States. A deal on the construction of the new United States military sites was signed soon afterwards in May 1942. Panama had already declared war on Japan immediately after the attack on Pearl Harbor and on Germany and Italy a few days later. Panama was also active in helping the United States combat the threat from German submarines in the approaches to the Canal. In spite of the abrupt end to his Presidency, however, Arias was to remain a key figure in his country's politics until his death at the age of 87 in 1988.[8]

Despite American fears, the canal was not attacked during the war and afterwards the temporary bases were all due to revert back to Panama. An attempt by Washington to reach an agreement to keep hold of some of them for a number of years afterwards, however, provoked angry demonstrations among students and the idea was abandoned. Meanwhile the status of the Canal Zone continued to cause tensions between the two countries, despite the 1936 agreement. In 1952 Colonel José Antonio Rémon, a key figure behind the scenes in Panamanian politics since the ousting of Arias in 1941, began fresh negotiations over the status of the Canal Zone with Washington, which resulted in an agreement signed in 1955. This gave extra money to Panama, rights over tax income from the zone and other concessions, though the central issue of sovereignty was not resolved. Rémon did not live to see to see the agreement implemented, as he was gunned down at a horse racetrack in January 1955. The limitations of the new agreement with Panama were also highlighted in 1956 when Washington pointedly excluded the country from London talks to discuss the Suez Canal issue of that year.

The sovereignty issue was to sour relations between the two countries periodically for years to come. One of the worst episodes came in 1964 when American students at Balboa High School raised an American flag – but no Panamanian equivalent. Violence and riots erupted and for a brief period Panama broke off diplomatic relations with Washington. It would not be until 1977 that the two countries signed an agreement allowing sovereignty over the Canal to pass to Panama on 31 December 1999.

Nicaragua had enthusiastically ratified the Treaty of Versailles to become a League of Nations founding member on 3 November 1920 and sent its Chargé d'Affaires in Paris, Carlos A Villanueva, to be its delegate at its first General Assembly. Unlike its Central American neighbours, though in common with Haiti, Nicaragua became a full member of the League while having soldiers from a non-member – the United States – stationed on its soil to guarantee law and order.

The limitation in the reach of the League and the importance of the proximity of the United States to Nicaragua and other Central American states were shown once again in the events of 1922 and 1923. These involved another of the seemingly never-ending disputes concerning Nicaragua,

Honduras, and this time El Salvador, which for a while threatened war. The United States intervened to mediate, but Secretary of State Hughes, who had personally wanted his country to ratify the Treaty of Versailles and join the League, was keen that Washington try to arrange a more permanent system in the region to ensure peace. At the end of 1922 and through to early 1923 he hosted a conference of Central American countries at which no fewer than 13 different treaties were signed between the various countries – though only one directly involved the United States – on issues ranging from free trade to labour laws and transport. A key agreement among the Central American Republics was to refrain from intervening in the internal political affairs of neighbours – a constant source of problems in the region. The agreement also established a Central American tribunal, which was effectively a court of arbitration. The treaties were by no means guaranteed to produce peace in the region, and nor did they. But they did provide a blueprint for the handling of the Honduran crisis in 1923 when revolution broke out. They were also more relevant to most Central American nations than the grander but remote and ultimately toothless League of Nations. In common with many other nations Nicaragua eventually quit the League altogether, in 1936, though by then it and the legacy of the Paris Peace Conference had long ceased to be relevant to the country.

A key problem in Nicaragua in the 1920s was one that had persisted for decades, a chronic lack of political stability. The presence of American marines since 1912 may have helped keep the peace – mostly – but it did little to further the development of true democratic politics as warring factions – the Liberals, Conservatives and factions of both – vied to show that they were the ones with the support of the

Americans deemed crucial to win and maintain power in the country. The United States was thus in a quandary. Public opinion back home broadly supported the withdrawing of the marines, a policy that also fitted better with the move away from direct military intervention. Yet to withdraw the troops risked prompting yet more instability in a country that was still strategically important. Washington wanted both to ensure that no other country could build a rival canal through Nicaragua and maintain its option, if needed, to build a second one there itself.

The dilemma for Nicaragua and Washington was graphically illustrated when the marines were withdrawn in 1925 after free if not particularly fair elections were won by Liberal-Conservative coalition candidate Carlos Solórzano. Shortly afterwards the defeated candidate started a revolt and seized power. This was General Emiliano Chamorro, son of Paris Peace Conference delegate Salvador, who had meanwhile returned to his post as President of the country's National Assembly. General Chamorro ignored warnings from Washington that it would not recognise his government. The Liberals staged a counter-rebellion and eventually in 1926 Chamorro felt obliged to step down as President. However by this time, with Mexico publicly backing the Liberal cause, Washington decided that it would be prudent to send the marines back in. The former President – and loyal friend of the United States – Adolfo Díaz was temporarily in charge of the country while a peace treaty between the Conservatives and Liberals was negotiated under American supervision in 1927.

Two key aspects of this agreement were to have far-reaching consequences for the future of Nicaragua. One was that the Americans insisted on the creation of a National Guard to replace the armed forces. The aim was to build a non-partisan body that would act as a reassurance to all political sides, thus encouraging them not to take up arms themselves if and when they lost an election. Its officers were to be trained by the Americans. The other factor was the failure to sign the Treaty on the part of one of the Liberal military leaders. That person's name was Augusto César Sandino. Rejecting the agreement, he took to the hills in the north of the country with a group of 30 men to oppose it.

The long-term consequences of these two factors were not immediately apparent. Most of the Liberals accepted the new accord, and the Americans felt confident they would soon be able to withdraw their marines for good. The 1928 elections had been won fairly, if narrowly, by General José María Moncada, Sandino's old boss, followed by victory for another Liberal Juan Bautista Sacasa. Though Sacasa's win was admittedly an embarrassment for the Americans – whose allies had generally been the Conservatives – it was not enough to worry the United States into keeping their troops on Nicaraguan soil. The country at least had an air of stability. Yes, Sandino was undefeated and an irritant, but he was not regarded as a major threat to the country.

THE CHAMORRO NAME
It was perhaps appropriate that a document as historic as the Treaty of Versailles should have been signed by someone bearing the name Chamorro. For Salvador Chamorro was one in a long line, both before and since, in his family to have a major influence on Nicaraguan public life and politics. In 1921, for example, the government run by President Diego Manuel Chamorro contained no fewer than twelve members of the family as ministers or officials, ranging from the Minister of the Interior to the Consul in London, and including Salvador Chamorro himself as President of the country's Congress. In more recent times Violeta Chamorro, who married into the family, became President in 1990, twelve years after her husband Pedro Joaquín Chamorro was assassinated.

Meanwhile, domestic pressure in the United States was also growing to bring the marines home. One reason was the cost of keeping them there at a time when the Depression was beginning to bite. The state of the world economy was also a strategic factor behind the marines leaving. International trade was down, thus there was no need to think that an additional canal across the isthmus would be needed in the foreseeable future. The last marine left at the start of 1933, amid considerable relief in Washington.

Sandino had continued fighting his war in the hills with his small but well drilled force known as the Ejército Defensor de la Soberanía Nacional de Nicaragua (EDSN). He saw the new American-trained National Guard as a major threat to Nicaraguan sovereignty. Though he often used Marxist rhetoric, and was certainly of the left, Sandino was not – as was sometimes claimed – a Communist but essentially a nationalist bitterly opposed to United States involvement in his country. To the Americans in Washington he may just have been a 'bandit', but to many people across the Latin American world Sandino was a hero, a man who had dared to take on the might of the United States and who, if he had not won, had at least not been defeated by its marines. In reality Sandino's position was a little more complicated. Though implacably opposed to American intervention, the old Bryan-Chamorro Treaty and the National Guard, the guerrilla had been a Liberal and the Liberals were now in charge under President Sacasa. Sympathisers of Sandino were now in government.

In 1933 there was an agreement between Sandino and Sacasa which in theory brought an end to the former's armed struggle. But tension remained, and in particular there were clashes between members of the now technically disbanded EDSN and the National Guard. In February 1934 Sandino went to Managua for talks with President Sacasa to resolve the tensions. However, as Sandino left the presidential palace on 21 February he and his aides were murdered by Guard members. This was no random shooting. The head of the National Guard was a ruthless and ambitious man called Anastasio 'Tacho' Somoza Garcia, himself a Liberal who was well connected among the landowning elite and who had the backing of many in Washington. The result of this brutal event was that Sandino became a martyred hero across Latin America while Somoza, who had given the orders to kill the guerrilla leader, was to emerge as the country's dominant political figure for the next twenty-two years.

Somoza formally seized power from Sacasa in 1936 and through the vehicle of his Partido Liberal Nacionalista became President in January 1937. At home Somoza consolidated his power base among the National Guard and the landowning elite, bringing in measures to stimulate agriculture in the country, encouraging banks to invest in new crops and opening up the country to foreign investment. At the same time he and his family amassed huge wealth, assuring they had not just political and military but financial clout in the country. By 1944 Somoza was said to own nearly a hundred ranches or plantations. He was also ruthless with opposition voices; though he allowed the Conservatives to continue to function, he never permitted them to become a serious threat, and he also controlled the press. The main opposition at this time was led by Emiliano Chamorro from outside the country. Diplomatically, the dictator reversed the traditional Nicaraguan Liberal mistrust of the United States and received both economic and later military aid from a grateful Washington. In 1939 he was accorded a state visit to Washington, an honour that sent an important message both around the world and to the Nicaraguan public and political classes that Somoza enjoyed the support of the American government.

Somoza was able to reward American backing during the Second World War when he quickly followed the United States in declaring war first on Japan then Germany, and allowed his ally to site bases in Nicaragua. Somoza's regime also helped the Americans supply fruit and vegetables to the Panama Canal Zone. The dictator meanwhile took advantage of the war to confiscate property once owned by Germans in Nicaragua for his own personal gain. This became the basis for much of his later wealth. He also brought a degree of prosperity to parts of the country.

In the 1930s Nicaragua had the lowest GDP or income per head in Central America but by the 1960s it was second only to Costa Rica. From 1949 to 1970 exports grew more than six fold, and the country's economy grew faster than any other Latin American country. Little of the wealth, however, trickled down to the poorer sections of society.

Somoza's grip on power in Nicaragua was tight, though not entirely without opposition. From time to time he faced challenges from dissident Liberals and Conservatives and even a challenge closer at home. In 1947 he put forward Leonardo Argüello as his official candidate, the man he had beaten in the 1936 poll. However Argüello proved more independently minded than expected and began moving officers around in the National Guard, the citadel of Somoza's support. Argüello was quickly removed and replaced by the dictator's uncle. This action earned the wrath of Washington which refused to recognise the government until an astute intervention by Nicaraguan forces in the civil war raging in Costa Rica saw the wily dictator finally get his way with the administration of President Harry S Truman. Somoza had himself elected President again in 1950 and remained in control until 1956 when he was assassinated. This was far from the end of the Somoza regime, however. The dictator had created his own dynasty and his two sons Luis Somoza and Anastasio 'Tachito' Somoza Debayle, both groomed for the job, kept the regime going until 1979 when it was toppled by the Frente Sandinista de Liberación Nacional (FSLN). This was named after Augusto César Sandino, the man murdered by 'Tacho' Somoza's henchmen.

8
Cuba and Haiti

For the people of Haiti, the immediate post-First World War period promised more of what they had endured since 1915 – occupation by American troops. The presence of the marines, who brought a measure of stability to a chaotically violent political system, was to dominate Haitian affairs until 1934. The choices faced by the people were stark and unenviable. If the marines left, there was risk of a return to the bloodletting that immediately preceded their arrival. But if they stayed, Haiti would effectively remain an American protectorate for the foreseeable future.

In Paris, Haiti's delegate Tertulien Guilbaud had used the Conference as an opportunity to meet senior American figures and press his country's case for, at least, a relaxation in the level of United States control. Ultimately this led to nothing; and Haiti's most concrete achievement as a result of the Conference was to ratify the Treaty of Versailles and become a founding member of the League of Nations – its membership was formally accepted on 30 June 1920. Guilbaud, the Chargé d'Affaires in Paris, was the man who handed over a copy of Haiti's ratification documents to be lodged at the Foreign Ministry in Paris. He was also a natural choice to be a delegate at the first General Assembly meeting in Geneva, where he was joined by Auguste Bonamy, who had been Chief Justice at the Court of Cassation in Port-au-Prince, and writer Fréderic Doret.

However, by the end of 1920 Guilbaud was already 64 years old and this was his last official post in the service of his country. The following April he was recalled to Haiti and on 24 May 1923, two days after his 67th birthday, he officially retired and was granted a pension. The writer and politician then lived in Port-au-Prince, though his quiet existence was rudely shattered by the death of his wife, Marie Victoire, in 1931. Five years later Guilbaud's pension was increased by a grateful state but he did not live much longer. On 19 September 1939 Guilbaud died peacefully at his home in the Haitian capital at the age of 83. He had lived just long enough to see the outbreak of a war which he and his fellow delegates had hoped to forestall when they had signed the Treaty of Versailles twenty years earlier and created the League of Nations. Guilbaud's beloved Haiti itself stayed in the organisation a little longer. When it finally left in April 1942 it was the last founding member to quit the League. Membership had hardly proved of great benefit to his country.

Among the many ignominies to be suffered by Haitians was the effective imposition of a new constitution on the country in 1918, following the US intervention three years earlier. One of the worst aspects of this US State Department-drafted constitution from the Haitian point of view was that it removed the existing prohibition on foreign land ownership – a sensitive issue in a nation built by former slaves. The man who later claimed to be the author of the constitution was Assistant Secretary of the United States Navy at the time, one Franklin

D Roosevelt. When the Haitian Congress refused to back an early draft of the constitution, President Dartiguenave dissolved it and held a plebiscite, which won approval.[1] Another major issue for Haitians was American control over the country's finances, including customs receipts.

Humiliating though these measures were, it was another more everyday and practical piece of domestic legislation revived by the Americans that sparked a major revolt in early 1919. The *corvée* was an old law that required peasants to give up part of their time to build roads. Given that at the start of the American occupation Haiti had just a few miles of roads outside the towns, it can be seen that this was a law that had fallen into desuetude. The law was revived to construct a few hundred miles of new road with some success. But for the peasants forced to take part, under the watchful supervision of armed guards, it felt more than a little like a return to slavery at the hands of white men. Soon there was rebellion in the air.

The so-called 'Caco Revolt' was named after the *cacos* who took part in it. These were peasant militias or fraternities who lived in the country's mountainous interior – estimates of their numbers range from a few thousand to tens of thousands. The *cacos* had devised secret signs so they could recognise each other, while another of their distinctive traits was that they blew conch shells when they went into battle. Over the years they had played a key role in Haitian politics, being recruited by successive presidential hopefuls as their own personal armies. The leader of the 1919 revolt, Charlemagne Peralte, was killed by marines, and in a bid to quell the uprising his body was photographed to let people see that he was dead. However the bloody revolt continued under another leader, Benoît Batraville, until it was finally brought to an end in1920. In all some 1,500 Haitians and around a dozen marines were killed.

The ferocity of the revolt and the way it was put down by American troops and the Haiti Guard – a militia created at the request of Washington – raised concern not just in Haiti but back in the United States too. Some have subsequently referred to the 1915–22 period as America's 'Black Vietnam'. A Senate investigation cleared American marines of any widespread wrongdoing, but there were damaging public allegations of 'indiscriminate killings' by some soldiers. On the other side there were also gruesome stories of marines being killed and their bodies horribly mutilated, and even one lurid allegation that the body parts of one officer were eaten. In May 1921 a delegation of senior Haitian figures went to Washington with a memo outlining the result of six years of occupation and making allegations of torture, theft, ballot rigging and ill-treatment of prisoners by American troops. The three delegates described the occupation as the 'most terrible regime of military autocracy which has ever been carried out in the name of the great American democracy'.[2]

The outcome of these events, however, was not the withdrawal of American troops but instead a shake-up in the way Washington ran Haiti. The position of High Commissioner was created in 1922 and the man appointed was General John H Russell, until then the head of the Marine Corps in Haiti and the man who had passed on confidential documents from the Haitians to the American delegation during the Paris Peace Conference. He and President Louis Borno ran Haiti in tandem for the rest of the decade. It was a period of some material progress in the country. New roads were built, new crops were introduced to boost agricultural efficiency and diversity, and health and sanitation were improved. Foreign debt repayments were also maintained and the country experienced relative stability. Discontent among the Haitian populace over American occupation continued, however, and as economic conditions worsened after 1929 the clamour for action grew. In December of that year a number of Haitians, protesting against economic conditions, were gunned down by marines at Cayes. This prompted US President Herbert Hoover to call for a commission of inquiry into the situation in Haiti.

The Forbes Commission, as it was known, praised much of the work that the Americans had done in health and sanitation and other matters but was critical over the lack of involvement of Haitians in key administrative roles. It recommended the abolition of the position of High Commissioner, the use of more local officials in government, the phased withdrawal of the marines and an amendment of treaty agreements between the two countries to reduce American involvement. It was clear that Washington wanted to remove itself from Haiti as fast as it safely could. Partly this was for laudable reasons – the occupation of the country simply looked and felt anachronistic. Partly it was for more practical reasons; occupation was a drain on finances at a time of economic crisis.

The negotiations were long and protracted over how to define the exact nature of the new relationship between the two countries. The main sticking point was money: the United States did not want to relinquish its firm grip on Haiti's finances. By now Roosevelt had taken office, a figure mistrusted in Haiti because of his authorship of the 1918 Constitution. On the Haitian side the new elected ruler was President Sténio Vincent, who had been one of the three delegates who went to Washington in 1921 to complain about the occupation. Like his predecessors under American occupation, he was mixed-race or mulatto rather than black, another source of grievance for many Haitians. The majority black population of the country resented the clear preference the Americans showed for the minority mulattos over them.

Bypassing the Haitian Congress that was opposed to it, the two Presidents reached an agreement in 1933 that allowed for the withdrawal of marines and the gradual relinquishing of control over Haiti's financial affairs. On 15 August 1934 the last American marines left, ending 19 years of an occupation that by common consent, and notwithstanding some limited achievements, had been damaging both for the United States and particularly Haiti.[3]

The end of occupation did not mean Haiti's troubles with its near neighbours were over. For many years there had been tensions between the two neighbours on the island of Hispaniola, especially over the number of Haitian migrant workers in the Dominican Republic. On occasions the border was closed and tensions often ran high. In October 1937 the Dominican Republic dictator President Rafael Trujillo, claiming that Haiti was harbouring his political enemies, ordered his troops to round up Haitian workers. Thousands of them were massacred – perhaps as many as 20,000 or more. Following an international investigation of the atrocity, and under pressure from Washington, Trujillo eventually agreed to pay Haiti compensation for the killings.

Though European influence in Haiti had been reduced as a result of its occupation, the United States was still anxious to ensure that the country did not fall under the influence of outside powers after the start of the Second World War. Haiti was quick to declare war on Japan and by 12 December 1941 had also declared against Germany and Italy too. Then, in April 1942, Haiti agreed to allow the US Navy to locate a patrol base in the west of the country to help safeguard the Windward Passage. After the war Haiti signed a Military Assistance Agreement with the United States, whose concern had by then switched from potential Nazi aggression to the perceived Soviet threat.

The ongoing racial tension in Haiti resurfaced in 1946 when, during mounting economic problems, the mulatto President Élie Lescot was ousted by the Haitian Guard and a black politician Dumarsais Estimé was installed as President. He moved to replace mulattos in the bureaucracy with black officials, and oversaw reforms aimed at helping the conditions of both rural and urban workers. The foreign debt was also paid off after the raising of what was called the *Libération Financière* Loan in 1947. However, though Estimé enjoyed some popularity with the public, his rule was not to be the start of a new period of stability in Haitian politics that so many longed for. In 1950 he tried to change the Constitution so he could remain in power. The move was opposed by a majority of the Senate and eventually the army intervened and deposed the President.

The new man in charge was a military officer, Colonel Paul Magloire, the son of a general, who had been involved in the 1946 plot to get rid of Lescot. Though black, Magloire enjoyed the support of the country's small but influential mulatto elite. He proved a popular President in many ways, overseeing a growth period in coffee exports, bringing in votes for women and backing a number of irrigation projects. Magloire, who was notably anti-Communist, also enjoyed good relations with the United States. However a combination of ambitious rivals and a scandal over the theft of relief funds raised after the devastation of Hurricane Hazel in 1954 helped seal his fate; and in 1956, faced with strikes and demonstrations, he fled into exile.

The stage was now set for the arrival of one of the grimmest and most damaging periods in Haitian history. In 1957 a rigged election saw François Duvalier become President. 'Papa Doc' Duvalier, as he is best known, had studied medicine and had been named head of the health service in 1946 before becoming Minister of Health in 1949. Ruthlessly ambitious, he set about ruling Haiti with absolute authority, creating a special police force known as the Tonton macoutes, or 'bogey men', to make sure his will was enforced. Duvalier tapped into the growing resentment of the black population against mulatto influence in Haiti and also studied the country's native religion Voodoo (usually spelt Vodou in Haiti), knowledge he used to gain popularity with many ordinary Haitians. Thousands of people are said to have been murdered under the Duvalier regime; some say up to 30,000. In 1961 the United States suspended economic aid to Haiti because of the dictator's behaviour. However it was restored a year later when Haiti helped the United States vote to keep Cuba out of the Organisation of American States. Duvalier ruled until his death in 1971, but even then there was little respite for the country. He was replaced by his son Jean-Claude 'Baby Doc' Duvalier.

ALL-AMERICAN COOPERATION
The desire to have an all-American structure through which the countries of the continent could meet to discuss and resolve problems stretches back to the First American Conference of States held in Washington in 1889 to create the International Union of American Republics. In 1920 this became the Union of American Republics and its permanent office was called the Pan American Union. In 1948 at the Ninth American Conference of States in Bogotá it was agreed to establish a new body which became the Organisation of American States, or OAS. Its charter came into being in 1951.

Cuba's delegate to the Paris Peace Conference, Dr Antonio Sánchez de Bustamante y Sirvén, had played a productive if low key role in the peace negotiations. In particular, the international lawyer had been a member of the body to discuss international labour legislation, one of the less glamorous but more productive of the conference's Commissions. This Commission had been set up in response to the growing chorus at the end of the war from trade unions and other workers' bodies in the Western world for better rights and conditions, and was given added impetus by the revolution in Russia. Its aim was to set minimum standards for rights and conditions for workers around the world, for example on hours of work, sickness benefits and the protection of children. As a result of the Commission's work the first International Labour Conference was held in Washington in October 1919, at which six International Labour Conventions were adopted. The International Labour Organisation itself was based in Geneva from 1920, under the directorship of Frenchman Albert Thomas.

However, Bustamante's real expertise was in international private law, which regulates trade and the movement of goods, services and people between different countries. His ability had already led to his being appointed in 1908 to the Permanent Court of Arbitration in The Hague, set up after the first Hague Conference of 1899. In 1921 Bustamante was made a permanent member of that court and also appointed as a judge to the new Permanent Court of International Justice (predecessor of the International Court of Justice) set up under Article 14 of the League of Nations Covenant. Bustamante emerged as an important figure on the Court, and was re-elected to it in 1930. In 1925 he wrote a book about the body simply entitled *The World Court*.

In the book Bustamante shows he had a very clear idea of how such a court should and should not operate on the world scene. For example, there had been proposals that the Court be allowed to offer advisory opinions on matters of law posed by any state or group of states. Bustamante, however, immediately saw the dangers of such an approach. These proposals would have *done much harm to the work of the Court* and *would have made it possible to bring before the Court under the guise of advisory opinions disputes which the other party did not want to submit to the Court in the form of a litigation; it would have been a clever way of finding out what the Court's decision would be in a subsequent litigation or of learning what would be the best reasons for refusing to compromise or arbitrate the question.*[4]

The book is an erudite work, casting back to Greek and Roman writers in an attempt to shed light on contemporary legal philosophy. For the most part it is an explanation of the workings of the Court, with Bustamante providing the context and background for its functioning, as well as a discussion of the cases it had already heard. But the book also gives us glimpses of the lawyer's optimism and humanity. Referring to the Court's creation, he says, ... *the writer [Bustamante], bolder every day in his hope for its future, desires to repeat ... it is no small thing for our generation to have witnessed its birth and to have seen it take its seat.* The author also muses on the paradox that the Court had only come about because of a bloody conflict. *Without the World War ... the governments would never have decided to put it into practice. That is human nature. It learns from preaching and from logic, but still more from unhappiness and grief.* He concludes the book: ... *let us celebrate the fact that at last between nations, as for a long time between men, we can now, under the protection of a Permanent Court, speak of law and of justice, for the strong and the weak.*[5]

Bustamante's greatest contribution to world jurisprudence, however, was not his work at the International Court but in the development of private international law throughout the Americas. As long ago as 1877 a congress in Lima, Peru had sought to establish a single code of international law that would apply throughout the continent, with the aim of improving trade, the movement of goods and services and of reducing the number of disputes by having an agreed framework under which such deals could operate. This is an area sometimes known as the conflict of laws. The Cuban lawyer laboured on such a framework of laws and in 1928 the Sixth International Conference of American States in Havana – of which he was President – agreed to adopt his lengthy work. Consisting of four parts covering civil, commercial, criminal and procedural law, it became officially known as the Bustamante Code and was later described as the 'the most important codification of the rules of the conflict of laws in force'. Years later

> We can now, under the protection of a Permanent Court, speak of law and of justice, for the strong and the weak.
> **ANTONIO SÁNCHEZ DE BUSTAMANTE, 1925**

another academic remarked: 'No work can now be written on the subject of private international law without constant and frequent references to the Bustamante Code.' In all, some fifteen Latin American countries ratified it.[6]

Bustamante was in demand in academia and spent part of 1929 lecturing at Emory University in Atlanta, Georgia, and had earlier spent time in Chicago. In the 1930s he also published a three-volume work on private international law which further enhanced his reputation as one of the leading experts in his field. After his time in The Hague Bustamante eventually retired to Havana, though without his wife Isabel who had died some years before. The lawyer, who had two sons, finally died at his home in the Cuban capital on 24 August 1951 at the age of 86. A natural optimist and believer in the power of international law, he had thus lived through not one but two World Wars. Back in 1908 he had written: *To be neutral today is the right of all nations, not derived from the consent of the belligerents, but rather imposed upon them absolutely. War is an abnormal condition, occurs at increasingly greater intervals, and is becoming of shorter and shorter duration.* It is unlikely he still held the same view by the time of his death more than four decades later.[7]

Bustamante died well before the momentous events that were to rock both Cuba and the world in 1959. Instead he had been able to witness his home country exist under first a de facto American protectorate and then under a form of economic hegemony established by its large neighbour. It was a period in which Cuba's great economic attribute – its huge sugar industry – was to prove both a blessing and a curse.

Immediately after the First World War, a shortage of sugar in the world pushed up prices, leading to a mini boom in Cuba with prices reaching 22.5 cents a pound. Then, as other sources of sugar came back into production the value of the crop plummeted, reaching 4 cents just seven months later. As was often the case with Central American and Caribbean countries in the first half of the 20th century, an over-dependence on one main agricultural export made Cuba dangerously vulnerable to sudden changes in world trade. This weakness was not helped by the fact that Cuba's sugar industry became increasingly reliant on the United States, whose economy was to suffer a crippling blow in 1929. Fluctuations in prices and the quality of harvests also made for a volatile situation among Cuba's rural and urban workers, both of whom largely depended on the sugar industry for their livelihoods.

Politically there was little sign of lasting stability. In 1921 Washington felt obliged to invoke the Platt Amendment – under which the United States had a right to intervene to maintain security on the island – after the defeated candidate refused to accept the results of the 1920 presidential elections. A mission headed by General Enoch Crowder was dispatched to the island. The mission lasted two years and brought a degree of stability under President Alfredo Zayas, as well as beginning to tackle some of the economic problems and corruption that continued to dog the island. Yet the intervention, the last of its kind under the Platt Amendment, was to change little in the long term. In 1924 Gerardo Machado y Morales was elected President, the start of a particularly brutal period in the country's history. Machado engineered his own re-election in 1928 and his rule was characterized by repression of all opposition and corruption. His tyrannical rule in turn inspired widespread opposition from students, workers and the middle classes, a situation exacerbated by the fall in sugar prices after the start of the Depression. Bombings and murder were said to be daily occurrences, and according to one writer 'a veritable reign of terror existed in Cuba' by the start of the 1930s. Despite the mounting chaos the Americans decided not to intervene, though in 1933 the newly-elected President Roosevelt sent a senior official to Havana to help 'ease out Machado'.[8]

Machado eventually fled in August of that year after a general strike and widespread popular protests. Cuba now seemed on the verge of major and radical change, even more so when a few weeks after being established the new provisional government was overthrown. The two key men in this latest coup were a left-leaning academic Dr Ramón Grau San Martín and a young army sergeant called Fulgencio Batista. Soviets or workers councils were set up and a socialist revolution seemed imminent, much to the alarm of Washington where some – though crucially not Roosevelt or his Secretary of State – favoured armed intervention. However, it was the new government itself that changed the situation when the pragmatic Batista ousted Grau. Batista proposed Colonel Carlos Mendieta as President, an altogether more palatable candidate to the Americans. The crisis was averted, and in January 1934 Washington finally recognised the new government and US Navy warships were pulled back from Cuban waters.

The Roosevelt Administration moved quickly to cement the position of the new Cuban government, now that the revolutionary mood – for the time being – had passed. It signed a new treaty with Havana that ended the much-despised Platt Amendment, while signing a new trade deal to boost the island's ailing economy and protect the country's sugar industry. In a sense political and military hegemony was replaced by economic dependence. As Cuban sugar flowed into the United States – up to 3 million tons a year – so too did American exports flood into Cuba with the help of loans and credit provided to Havana. In 1933 Cuban imports from its neighbour were worth $22.7 million. By 1941 this would jump to $147 million and to $617.9 million in 1957.

After removing Grau, Batista was to be the major figure in Cuban politics for the next 25 years, sometimes as President – from 1940 to 1944 – more often through placemen presidents and finally as dictator after 1952. It was a pattern of government familiar to Cubans; a ruthless strongman in charge, corruption and heavy economic dependency on the United States and the sugar industry. Under Batista, Cuba was quick to declare war on the Axis powers in December 1941 and later the next year it granted the United States facilities on the island to carry out operation against German submarines. Meanwhile Cuba's output of sugar doubled. After the war the Cuban government signed a Mutual Defense Agreement with the United States as an anti-Communist measure that also brought in cash for military use.

The controlling nature of Batista's regime and its usually cosy relationship with the United States did little to suggest that Cuban history was about to undergo a major transformation any time in the immediate future. Business as usual seemed the order of the day after the Second World War. However, by the early 1950s revolutionaries were plotting the overthrow of the Batista regime. The first attempt was a complete fiasco. On 26 July 1953 a young man named Fidel Castro and his brother Raul staged an assault on army barracks in the south of the island. Half the group of 170 or so were killed or arrested, and eventually the two brothers felt obliged to give themselves up. They were both given long jail terms and that could have been the end of the matter. However Batista, looking to improve his image, issued a general amnesty, and Fidel Castro headed to Mexico where he plotted his next move.

It was on 2 December 1956 that the two Castros and Ernesto Guevara – better known as 'Che' and who had been in Guatemala when the CIA had helped depose President Arbenz – arrived in the yacht *Granma* and landed with around eighty men to begin their latest assault on the Cuban regime. They immediately headed straight to the rugged Sierra Maestra, and so began one of the most famous revolutionary struggles in 20th century history. It was certainly not straightforward or inevitable.

In 1957 Castro had under his control a small force – perhaps never more than a thousand men in the early months – and the campaign made little apparent headway. The hope had been to exploit urban uprisings, but despite Batista's growing repression and brutality there was little sign of a decisive breakthrough. In 1958, however, the tide began to turn. In March of that year the Americans, under mounting pressure over their perceived support for Batista, announced a prohibition on supplying arms to either side. The move hit the Cuban regime not just militarily but psychologically. Sections of the armed forces began to doubt they could win. The rest of the year saw fierce guerrilla fighting from the rebels followed by a last-ditch attempt to regain some credibility by Batista when he held another election. Many Cubans abstained, a further sign that the dictator's authority was waning fast. Almost without warning on 1 January 1959 Batista, realising his days were numbered, flew off with family members to exile in the Dominican Republic. The Cuban Revolution had succeeded and Fidel Castro was now master of the island, a position he would maintain into the 21st century.

Epilogue

The participation of Cuba, Guatemala, Haiti, Honduras, Nicaragua and Panama in the Paris Peace Conference of 1919 did not attract much public attention, then or subsequently. The contribution of these nations to the workings of the Conference, while not absolutely negligible, was hardly significant. Yet it would be a mistake to see their involvement at Paris as wholly irrelevant from their point of view.

On one very practical level it was a rare chance for the six small countries to be involved in a momentous international event. More importantly, from the perspective of these countries the Conference should be seen not in the context of a European war and post-war settlement but as an extension of Central American and Caribbean regional politics. These countries had very few cards to play when it came to dealing with the dominant regional power, the United States. Thanks to its political clout, military might and economic muscle, it was Washington that held all the aces.

The six small powers thus saw Paris as an unusual opportunity to fight their corner in relation to the United States in an international setting. Having been 'rewarded' for backing the United States in the First World War with a place at the

Conference table, these smaller states did not want to squander that chance. To an extent, President Wilson had played into their hands. By championing the cause of self-determination, the rights of smaller nations and by promoting the League of Nations, the President had given the six states some ammunition to fire back at him. Surely, they argued, the fine ideals espoused in Wilson's rousing vision of international affairs applied just as much to Central America and the Caribbean as the rest of the world? If so, this meant that Washington had to show more restraint and understanding in its dealing with that region's smaller powers.

The representatives of these countries were not diplomatically naïve. Yes, they knew that attempts to persuade and embarrass the United States in an international gathering could perhaps bring some short-term gains. But they also knew, from long experience, that once the delegates' suitcases had been packed they would be left once more to deal with Washington alone, away from the glare of the world's media. That was why the League of Nations mattered to Cuba, Guatemala, Haiti, Honduras, Nicaragua and Panama. Not out of idealism, but as a practical and above all permanent way of curbing American intervention. The League provided a set of rules that all its members had to abide by, no matter how powerful they were.

This explains the importance of the failure of the United States to join the League. At a stroke, it rendered many of the Treaty of Versailles' achievements irrelevant from a Central American and Caribbean point of view. A League without Washington became little more than a high-minded talking shop unable to intervene in the one issue that really affected these six countries – their relations with the United States.

For if there was one thing that these small countries had

learnt since independence, and especially since the second half of the 19th century, it was that when it came to international politics, geography really did count. Fate had decreed that the six would always have the US as their near neighbour. It was once famously said of another country in the region: 'Poor Mexico, so far from God, and so close to the United States.'[1] At least part of that sentiment can also be said to apply to Cuba, Guatemala, Haiti, Honduras, Nicaragua and Panama.

Notes

Preface

1. Alfred Thayer Mahan, 'The United States Looking Outward', *Atlantic*, December 1890.

Chapter 1: Origins 1800–1900

1. Ralph Lee Woodward Jr, *Central America: A Nation Divided* (Oxford University Press, Oxford: 1985) p 94, hereafter Woodward, *Central America*.
2. Ibid, p 112.
3. Lester D Langley and Thomas David Schoonover, *Banana Men: American Mercenaries and Entrepreneurs in Central America* (University of Kentucky Press, Kentucky: 1995) p 56, hereafter Langley and Schoonover, *Banana Men*.
4. www.monografias.com/trabajos57/presidentes-honduras/presidentes-honduras2.shtml
5. Jenny Pearce, *Under the Eagle: US intervention in Central America and the Caribbean* (South End Press, London: 1981) p 9, hereafter Pearce, *Under the Eagle*.
6. *New York Times*, 11 March 1896.

7. 'John Brown' published in *Patrie*, 1885; and in Léon-François Hoffmann, 'Les Etats-Unis et les Américains dans les lettres haïtiennes' in *Études littéraires*, Vol 13, No. 2, 1980, pp 289–312.

Chapter 2: The Age of Interventions 1900–1914

1. Dana G Munro, *Intervention and Dollar Diplomacy in the Caribbean 1900–1921* (Princeton University, Princeton: 1964) p 87, hereafter Munro, *Intervention*.
2. Pearce, *Under the Eagle*, p 10.
3. Munro, *Intervention*, p 25.
4. Hans Schmidt, *Maverick Marine: General Smedley D. Butler and the Contradictions of American Military History* (University Press of Kentucky, Kentucky: 1987) p 40.
5. Quote from James N Cortada and James W Cortada, *US Foreign Policy in the Caribbean, Cuba and Central America* (Praeger, New York: 1986) p 67, hereafter Cortada and Cortada, *US Foreign Policy*; see also Schmidt, *Maverick Marine*, pp 40–41 on the involvement of the marines.
6. Alberto Acereda, *Rigoberto Guevara, Modernism, Rubén Darío, and the Poetics of Despair* (University Press of America, New York: 2004) p 327.
7. Langley and Schoonover, *Banana Men*, p 56.
8. Langley and Schoonover, *Banana Men*, p 57; see also *New York Times*, 15 January 1911.
9. *New York Times*, 15 January 1911 and 25 September 1910.
10. *New York Times*, 15 January 1911.
11. *New York Times*, 15 January 1911.
12. *New York Times*, 12 February 1912.

13. *The Times*, 3 December 1908.

Chapter 3: Follow My Leader 1914–1918

1. Percy Martin, *Latin America and the War* (John Hopkins Press, Baltimore: 1925) p 4, hereafter Martin, *Latin America and the War*.

2. Richard Smith, *Jamaican Volunteers in the First World War: Race, Masculinity and the Development of National Consciousness* (University of Manchester, Manchester: 2010) p 37.

3. *New York Times*, 8 May 1922.

4. Hans Schmidt, *The United States Occupation of Haiti 1915–1934* (Rutgers University Press, New Jersey: 1971) pp 93 and 95.

5. Information and quotation supplied to author by Bibliothèque Nationale d'Haïti.

6. Martin, *Latin America and the War*, pp 292–495.

7. Martin, *Latin America and the War*, pp 532–36.

8. See Martin, *Latin America and the War*, pp 520–41 for full details on the spies and propaganda.

9. *New York Times*, 9 March 1917.

10. Martin, *Latin America and the War*, p 492.

11. Martin, *Latin America and the War*, p 497.

13. Public Record Office, London CAB/24/3.

13. Charles H Harris III and Louis R Sadler, *The Archaeologist was a Spy: Sylvanus G. Morley and the Office of Naval Intelligence* (University of New Mexico Press, Albuquerque: 2003), p 134.

14. Thomas David Schoonover, *The French in Central America, Culture and Commerce 1820–1930* (Scholarly Resources, Delaware: 2000) p 142, hereafter Schoonover, *The French in Central America*.

15. Martin, *Latin America and the War*, pp 486–88.
16. Martin, *Latin America and the War*, pp 503–5.
17. *New York Times*, 16 January 1914.

Chapter 4: Getting Heard 1918–1919

1. United States Department of State, *The Paris Peace Conference*, Washington, DC, Vol I (US Government Printing Office, 1919) pp 225, 347–8; hereafter USDS, *The Paris Peace Conference*.
2. USDS, *Paris Peace Conference, 1919*, Vol I, pp 354–5.
3. USDS, *Paris Peace Conference, 1919*, Vol I, pp 304–7.
4. State Department document, Paris Peace Conference, 180.03101/2; hereafter SD-PPC.
5. SD-PPC, 180.03101/2.
6. SD-PPC, 183.9 Panama 1.
7. SD-PPC, 183.9 Panama 5.
8. SD-PPC, 183.9 Panama 5.
9. SD-PPC, 183.9 Panama 10.
10. SD-PPC, 183.9 Panama 12; SD-PPC, 183.9 Panama 36.
11. SD-PPC, 183.9 Honduras/2.
12. SD-PPC, 183.9 Guatemala/3.
13. Schoonover, *The French in Central America*, pp 145–7.
14. SD-PPC, 183.9 Nicaragua/1.
15. SD-PPC, 183.9 Honduras/ 1A.
16. SD-PPC, 183.9 Costa Rica 1; Paris Peace Conference, F.W. 180.03101/2; Schoonover, *The French in Central America* pp 148–9.
17. SD-PPC, 183.9, Costa Rica 2; SD-PPC, 183.9 Costa Rica 4.
18. Schoonover, *The French in Central America*, p 149.
19. SD-PPC, 183.9, Panama 5; SD-PPC, 819.00/1.
20. SD-PPC, 819.00/1.

21. SD-PPC, 819.00/1.
22. Preliminary Peace Conference protocol No 5, 180.0201/5, pp 19–25; hereafter Preliminary Protocol.
23. Preliminary Protocol, p 20
24. Preliminary Protocol, pp 21, 23.
25. Preliminary Protocol, p 25.
26. Preliminary Protocol, p 27.
27. Preliminary Protocol, p 28.
28. Preliminary Protocol, p 26; see also Martin, *Latin America and the War*, pp 504–5.

Chapter 5: Unhappy in Paris 1919

1. SD-PPC, 183.9 Haiti/1.
2. SD-PPC, 183.9 Haiti/1.
3. SD-PPC, 183.9 Haiti/1; *The Journal of American History*, Vol 88, No 3 (December 2001) pp. 882–7.
4. SD-PPC, 183.9 Haiti/1
5. SD-PPC, 183.9 Haiti/1
6. SD-PPC, 183.9 Haiti/1; SD-PPC, 183.9 Haiti/3
7. Munro, *Intervention*, pp 379–80.
8. Legación del Uruguay en Paris, 82/919; 94/919.
9. Paris Peace Conference, 180.03601/1, p 451; hereafter PPC
10. PPC, 180.03601/1, p 452.
11. PPC, 180.03601/1, p 452.
12. PPC, 180.03601/1, p 463.
13. PPC, 183.9, Cuba/4.
14. PPC, 183.9, Panama/19.
15. PPC, 182/68, p 37.
16. PPC, 182/68, p 37.
17. PPC, FO Delegation letter, 28 April 1919.
18. PPC, 183.9, Cuba/10.

19. PPC, 180.0201/6, p 50.

Chapter 6: Honduras and Guatemala

1. Elmer Bendiner, *A Time for Angels* (Alfred A Knopf, New York: 1975) p 163, hereafter Bendiner, *Angels*.
2. J. Lloyd Mecham, *A Survey of United States-Latin American Relations* (Houghton Miflin, New York: 1965) p 103, hereafter Mecham, *Survey*.
3. Schoonover, *The French in Central America*, p 152.
4. *New York Times*, 21 July 1921.
5. Bendiner, *Angels*, p 232.
6. Woodward, *Central America*, p 216.
7. Leslie Bethell (ed), *Central America Since Independence* (Cambridge University Press, Cambridge: 1991) p 126.

Chapter 7: Panama and Nicaragua

1. *New York Times*, 20 March 1921.
2. *New York Times*, 20 March 1921; *New York Times* 21 June 1921.
3. *New York Times*, 21 June 1921.
4. *New York Times*, 21 June 1921.
5. *New York Times*, 23 July 1922.
6. Mecham, *Survey*, pp 115–16.
7. Bendiner, *Angels*, p 248.
8. *Panama News*; http://www.hartford-hwp.com/ archives/47/353.html.

Chapter 8: Cuba and Haiti

1. Mecham, *Survey*, p 273.
2. *New York Times*, 16 October 1920; 4 January 1921; 9 May 1921.

3. See, for example, Cortada and Cortada, *US Foreign Policy*, p 77.
4. Antonio S de Bustamante (trans. Elizabeth F. Read), *The World Court* (The American Foundation, New York: 1925) p 255.
5. Ibid, pp 320–1.
6. G A L Droz, 'L'harmonisation des regles de conflits de lois et de jurisdictions dans les groupes regionaux d'Etats,' in *Rapports generaux aux VIe Congres international de droit compare* (Hamburg, 30 July–4 August 1962), p 399; *The American Journal of International Law*, Vol 45, No 4 (October 1951), p 747.
7. *The American Journal of International Law*, Vol 45, No 4 (October 1951), p 748.
8. Mecham, *Survey*, p 303.

Epilogue

1. Thomas E Skidmore and Peter H Smith, *Modern Latin America* (Oxford University Press, New York, 1988) p 217.

Chronology

YEAR	THE LIVES AND THE LANDS
1804	Haiti achieves independence from France.
1821	Guatemala, Honduras, El Salvador, Costa Rica declare independence from Spain.
	Panama declares independence from Spain, is part of Gran Colombia (later Colombia).
1822	Central American nations briefly annex themselves to Mexico.
1823	Central American countries declare complete independence as United Provinces of Central America.

YEAR	HISTORY	CULTURE
1804	Napoleon Bonaparte proclaimed Emperor, crowned in presence of Pope Pius VII in Paris.	English Water Colour Society founded. Ludwig van Beethoven, Symphony No 3 in E-flat minor, Op. 55 (*Eroica*).
1821	James Monroe begins 2nd term as US President. Napoleon Bonaparte dies. King George IV of Britain crowned.	*Manchester Guardian* founded. Percy Bysshe Shelley, *Adonais*. James Mill, *Elements of Political Economy*.
1822	Turkey invade Greece. Brazil becomes independent of Portugal.	Aleksandr Pushkin, *Eugene Onegin*. Royal Academy of Music founded in London.
1823	Mexico becomes republic. Monroe Doctrine 'declared'. Pope Leo XII succeeds Pope Pius VII.	Charles Macintosh invents waterproof fabric. James Fenimore Cooper, *The Pioneers*, 1st of *Leather-Stocking* novels.

YEAR	THE LIVES AND THE LANDS
1830–31	Panama twice, briefly, becomes independent from Colombia.
1837	Guatemala: Rafael Carrera leads peasant revolt on way to taking power.
1838	Nicaragua, Honduras, Costa Rica leave United Provinces of Central America, spelling its end.
1856	22 May Tertulien Marcelin Guilbaud born at Port-de-Paix, Haiti.

YEAR	HISTORY	CULTURE
1830–31	France captures Algeria. William IV becomes King of Britain. Charles X abdicates French throne; Louis-Philippe succeeds. Ecuador becomes independent of Gran Colombia. Poland declares independence from Russia. Belgium becomes independent of the Netherlands. Former US President James Monroe dies. Brazilian Emperor Pedro I abdicates, succeeded by son Pedro II.	Joseph Smith founds Mormon Church. Charles Darwin sails on *HMS Beagle* to South America, New Zealand and Australia. Great cholera pandemic originating from India (1826) spreads to Central Europe eventually reaching Scotland (1832). French Foreign Legion formed. Alfred Lord Tennyson, *Poems, Chiefly Lyrical*.
1837	Queen Victoria accedes to British throne. Constitutional revolts in Lower and Upper Canada.	Balzac, *Illusions perdus*. Thomas Carlyle, *The French Revolution*.
1838	Queen Victoria crowned. Battle of Blood River, Natal: Boers defeat Zulus. First Afghan War begins. First steamships cross Atlantic.	Elizabeth Barrett Browning, *The Seraphim and Other Poems*. National Gallery opens in London.
1856	Peace Conference in Paris recognises integrity of Ottoman Empire. Second Opium War begins.	Flaubert, *Madame Bovary*. Bell 'Big Ben' cast at Whitechapel Bell Foundry.

YEAR	THE LIVES AND THE LANDS
1857	Nicaragua: William Walker surrenders after attempt to take control.
1858	17 March José Policarpo Bonilla Vásquez born in Tegucigalpa, Honduras.
1861	Joaquín Méndez born in Guatemala.
1862	Haiti: US recognize independence.
1865	13 April: Antonio Sánchez de Bustamante y Sirvén born in Havana, Cuba.
1868	Cuba: start of Ten Years War independence movement; fails.

YEAR	HISTORY	CULTURE
1857	Indian Mutiny begins. Second Opium War. Garibaldi founds Italian National Association for unification of country.	Charles Baudelaire, *Les Fleurs du Mal*. Thomas Hughes, *Tom Brown's Schooldays*. Anthony Trollope, *Barchester Towers*. National Portrait Gallery, Victoria and Albert Museum open in London.
1858	Indian Mutiny ends: powers of East India Company transferred to British Crown. Suez Canal Company formed.	Thomas Carlyle, *Frederick the Great*. William P Frith, *Derby Day*.
1861	Confederate States of America formed: American Civil War begins. Italy declared kingdom under Victor Emmanuel II of Sardinia. Prince Albert of Britain dies.	Charles Dickens, *Great Expectations*. Fyodor Dostoesvsky, *The House of the Dead*. George Eliot, *Silas Marner*. Mrs Beeton, *Book of Household Management*.
1862	Otto von Bismarck becomes Prussian Prime Minister.	Ivan Turgenev, *Fathers and Sons*. Victor Hugo, *Les Misérables*.
1865	American Civil War ends: Thirteenth Amendment to US Constitution abolishes slavery. Transatlantic telegraph cable completed.	Lewis Carroll, *Alice's Adventures in Wonderland*. Richard Wagner, *Tristan und Isolde*.
1868	British Abyssinian expedition. Meiji Restoration in Japan. Ulysses S Grant elected US President.	Louisa May Alcott, *Little Women*. Wilkie Collins, *The Moonstone*. Richard Wagner, *Die Meistersinger von Nürnberg*

YEAR	THE LIVES AND THE LANDS
1871	11 May: Emiliano Chamorro Vargas born in Acoyapa, Nicaragua.
1873	11 February Antonio Burgos born in Panama.
1885	Haiti: Guilbaud publishes his best-known collection of poetry *Patrie*.
1889	Haiti: Guilbaud made member of Constituent Assembly that drafts new constitution.
1893	Nicaragua: José Santos Zelaya becomes dictator.
1894	Honduras: Manuel Bonilla becomes President.

YEAR	HISTORY	CULTURE
1871	Franco-Prussian War: Wilhelm I of Prussia declared German Emperor at Versailles; Treaty of Frankfurt ends war, ceding Alsace-Lorraine to Germany.	Lewis Carroll, *Through the Looking Glass*. George Eliot, *Middlemarch*. Charles Darwin, *The Descent of Man*. Giuseppe Verdi, *Aïda*.
1873	Republic proclaimed in Spain. Germans evacuate last troops from France. Famine in Bengal.	Leo Tolstoy, *Anna Karenina*. Walter Pater, *Studies in the History of the Renaissance*.
1885	General Gordon killed in fall of Khartoum to the Mahdi. The Congo becomes personal possession of King Léopold II of Belgium. Germany annexes Tanganyika and Zanzibar.	Guy de Maupassant, *Bel Ami*. H Rider Haggard, *King Solomon's Mines*. W S Gilbert and Arthur Sullivan, *The Mikado*.
1889	Austro-Hungarian Crown Prince Rudolf commits suicide at Mayerling. London Dock Strike.	Jerome K Jerome, *Three Men in a Boat*. Richard Strauss, *Don Juan*.
1893	Franco-Russian Alliance signed. France acquires protectorate over Laos. Benz constructs his four-wheel car.	Oscar Wilde, *A Woman of No Importance*. Art Nouveau appears in Europe. Giacomo Puccini, *Manon Lescaut*.
1894	Sino-Japanese War begins: Japanese defeat Chinese at Port Arthur. Dreyfus Case begins in France.	George & Weedon Grossmith, *The Diary of a Nobody*. Anthony Hope, *The Prisoner of Zenda*.

YEAR	THE LIVES AND THE LANDS
1895	Cuba: Start of new independence revolt; nationalist hero José Martí killed fighting Spanish troops.
1898	Guatemala: Manuel Estrada Cabrera takes power.
	Cuba: gains independence when Spanish-American War ends.
1899	Honduras: Bonilla stands down as President
	Creation of United Fruit Company (UFCO).
1900	Panama: Burgos publishes work on child psychology, first of many books on variety of subjects.
1901	Cuba: Platt Amendment sees Cuba become US protectorate.

YEAR	HISTORY	CULTURE
1895	Armenians massacred in Ottoman Empire. Jameson Raid into Transvaal. Marconi invents radio telegraphy.	H G Wells, *The Time Machine*. W B Yeats, *Poems*. Peter Tchaikovsky, *Swan Lake*.
1898	Dreyfus case: Zola publishes *J'Accuse* letter. Kitchener defeats Mahdists at Omdurman. Paris Métro opens. Bismarck dies.	Thomas Hardy, *Wessex Poems*. Henry James, *The Turn of the Screw*. Oscar Wilde, *The Ballad of Reading Gaol*.
1899	Anglo-Egyptian Sudan Convention. Second Boer War begins. First Peace Conference at the Hague.	Rudyard Kipling, *Stalky and Co*. Arthur Pinero, *Trelawny of the Wells*. Edward Elgar, *Enigma Variations*.
1900	Second Boer War: relief of Mafeking; capture of Johannesburg and Pretoria. King Umberto I of Italy assassinated. Boxer Rising in China.	Sigmund Freud, *The Interpretation of Dreams*. Giacomo Puccini, *Tosca*. Joseph Conrad, *Lord Jim*. Anton Chekhov, *Uncle Vanya*.
1901	Edward VII becomes King of Britain. US President William McKinley assassinated; succeeded by Theodore Roosevelt.	First five Nobel Prizes awarded. Thomas Mann, *Die Buddenbrooks*. Rudyard Kipling, *Kim*. Pablo Picasso's 'Blue Period' begins (–1905).

YEAR	THE LIVES AND THE LANDS
1902	Cuba: Bustamante becomes senator.
1903	Panama: declares independence from Colombia; quickly recognised by US. Honduras: Policarpo Bonilla becomes MP.
1904	Honduras: Policarpo Bonilla imprisoned; accused of plotting to overthrow Manuel Bonilla government. Roosevelt Corollary to Monroe Doctrine allows US to intervene in Central American failing states.
1906	Honduras: Bonilla released; goes to El Salvador.

YEAR	HISTORY	CULTURE
1902	Anglo-Japanese Treaty recognises independence of China and Korea. Treaty of Vereenigung ends Boer War. Triple Alliance between Austria, Germany and Italy renewed for another six years.	Arthur Conan Doyle, *The Hound of the Baskervilles.* Maxim Gorki, *Lower Depths.* Anton Chekhov, *Three Sisters.* Claude Monet, *Waterloo Bridge.*
1903	Entente Cordiale between France and Britain begins. Russian Social Democratic Party splits into Mensheviks and Bolsheviks (led by Lenin and Trotsky). Wright Brothers' first flight.	Henry James, *The Ambassadors.* G E Moore, *Principia Ethica.* George Bernard Shaw, *Man and Superman.* Jack London, *The Call of the Wild.* Anton Bruckner, *Symphony No. 9.*
1904	Entente Cordiale settles British–French colonial differences. Russo-Japanese War begins. Roosevelt wins US Presidential election.	J M Barrie, *Peter Pan.* Giacomo Puccini, *Madame Butterfly.* Anton Chekhov, *The Cherry Orchard.* Sigmund Freud, *The Psychopathology of Everyday Life.*
1906	British ultimatum forces Turkey to cede Sinai Peninsula to Egypt. Joao Franco becomes Prime Minister of Spain. Dreyfus rehabilitated in France. Earthquake in San Francisco, USA kills over 1,000.	John Galsworthy, *A Man of Property.* O Henry, *The Four Million.* Andre Derain, *Port of London.* Invention of first jukebox.

YEAR	THE LIVES AND THE LANDS
1907	Cuba: Bustamante heads delegation to Hague Conference; appointed to Permanent Court of Arbitration in The Hague the following year.
1909	Nicaragua: dictator José Santos Zelaya overthrown.
1911	Guatemala: Méndez appointed Minister to Washington
1912	Nicaragua: US send in marines, remain until 1933.
1913	Panama: Burgos appointed Minister to Spain.

YEAR	HISTORY	CULTURE
1907	British and French agree on Siamese independence. Peace Conference held in The Hague.	Joseph Conrad, *The Secret Agent*. Maxim Gorky, *Mother*. First Cubist exhibition in Paris. Pablo Picasso, *Les Demoiselles D'Avignon*.
1909	Britain's King Edward VII dies; succeeded by George V.	Puccini, *La Fanciulla del West*. R Vaughan Williams, *Sea Symphony*.
1911	German gunboat *Panther* arrives in Agadir; triggers international crisis. Italy declares war on Turkey.	Cubism becomes public phenomenon in Paris. D H Lawrence, *The White Peacock*. Richard Strauss, *Der Rosenkavalier*. Igor Stravinsky, *Petrushka*.
1912	*Titanic* sinks; 1,513 die. Montenegro declares war on Turkey. Turkey declares war on Bulgaria and Serbia. Woodrow Wilson elected US President. Armistice between Turkey, Bulgaria, Serbia and Montenegro.	Carl G Jung, *The Theory of Psychoanalysis*. Marc Chagall, *The Cattle Dealer*. Marcel Duchamp, *Nude descending a staircase II*. Arnold Schoenberg, *Pierrot Lunaire*.
1913	King George I of Greece assassinated; succeeded by Constantine I. Second Balkan War.	D H Lawrence, *Sons and Lovers*. Igor Stravinsky, *Le Sacre du Printemps*. Grand Central Station in New York completed.

YEAR	THE LIVES AND THE LANDS
1914	Panama Canal opens. First World War begins.
1915	Haiti: US send marines to quell unrest after President Vilbrun Guillaume Sam murdered; Guilbaud turns down offer of presidency. Guatemala: Méndez represents country at Panama-Pacific International Exposition in San Francisco.
1916	Nicaragua: Bryan-Chamorro Treaty with US; quickly leads to collapse of Central American Court of Justice. Haiti: Guilbaud appointed Minister to France.
1917	Nicaragua: Emiliano Chamorro becomes President. Panama and Cuba: 7 April, declare war on Germany; 10 December on Austria-Hungary. Honduras: May, severs relations with Berlin.

YEAR	HISTORY	CULTURE
1914	Archduke Franz Ferdinand of Austria-Hungary and wife assassinated in Sarajevo. First World War begins: Battles of Mons, the Marne and First Ypres: trench warfare on Western Front.	James Joyce, *Dubliners*. Theodore Dreiser, *The Titan*. Gustav Holst, *The Planets*. Henri Matisse, *The Red Studio*. Georges Braque, *Music*. Film: Charlie Chaplin in *Making a Living*.
1915	First World War: Battles of Neuve Chapelle and Loos; 'Shells Scandal', Gallipoli campaign; Germans sink British liner *Lusitania*, killing 1,198.	Joseph Conrad, *Victory*. John Buchan, *The Thirty-Nine Steps*.
1916	First World War: Battles of Verdun and the Somme. Wilson issues Peace Note to belligerents in European War.	Lionel Curtis, *The Commonwealth of Nations*. James Joyce, *Portrait of an Artist as a Young Man*. Claude Monet, *Waterlilies*. 'Dada' movement produces iconoclastic 'anti-art'.
1917	First World War: Nivelle offensive fails, mutinies in French army; Battle of Passchendaele (3rd Ypres). February Revolution in Russia. Zimmerman Telegram reveals German proposed provocation of Mexican action against US. 6 April: US declare war on Germany, 7 December, on Austria-Hungary. German and Russian delegates sign armistice at Brest-Litovsk.	T S Eliot, *Prufrock and Other Observations*. Pablo Picasso designs 'surrealist' costumes and set for Satie's *Parade*. Sergei Prokofiev, *Classical Symphony*.

YEAR	THE LIVES AND THE LANDS
1918	Nicaragua: March, declares war on Germany.
	Guatemala: 23 April, Méndez confirms to US media it is at war with Germany.
	Haiti: 13 July, declares war on Germany; new constitution imposed by US removes bar on foreign land ownership.
	Honduras: 19 July, declares war on Germany.
1919	Honduras: Policarpo Bonilla, chosen as delegate to Paris Peace Conference; requests clarification of Monroe Doctrine regarding Treaty of Versailles.
	Guatemala: Méndez chosen as delegate to Peace Conference.
	Haiti: Guilbaud chosen as delegate to Peace Conference; Charlemagne Peralte leads bloody but unsuccessful peasant revolt against United States occupation.
	Nicaragua: Salvador Chamorro chosen as delegate to Peace Conference; backs new League but stresses need for independence of Central American nations from US, suggests Federation of Central American countries.
	Cuba: Bustamante chosen as delegate to Peace Conference; influential on Commission on International Labour Legislation.
	Panama: Burgos chosen as delegate to Peace Conference.

YEAR	HISTORY	CULTURE
1918	First World War: German spring offensives fail.	Alexander Blok, *The Twelve.*
	Treaty of Brest-Litovsk between Russia and Central Powers.	Gerald Manley Hopkins, *Poems.*
		Luigi Pirandello, *Six Characters in Search of an Author.*
	Romania signs Peace of Bucharest with Germany and Austria-Hungary.	Bela Bartok, *Bluebeard's Castle.*
		Giacomo Puccini, *Il Trittico.*
	Ex-Tsar Nicholas II and family executed.	Oskar Kokoshka, *Friends* and *Saxonian Landscape.*
	Armistice signed between Allies and Germany.	Edvard Munch, *Bathing Man.*
	Kaiser Wilhelm II of German abdicates.	
1919	Communist Revolt in Berlin.	Bauhaus movement founded by Walter Gropius.
	Paris Peace Conference adopts principle of founding League of Nations.	Thomas Hardy, *Collected Poems.*
	Benito Mussolini founds Fascist movement in Italy.	George Bernard Shaw, *Heartbreak House.*
	Treaty of Versailles signed.	Film: *The Cabinet of Dr Caligari.*
	Irish War of Independence begins.	
	US Senate votes against ratification of Versailles Treaty, leaving US outside League of Nations.	

YEAR	THE LIVES AND THE LANDS
1920	Guatemala: Cabrera's long rule ends.
	Cuba: US invoke Platt Amendment for last time to bring stability to the island.
1921	Policarpo Bonilla named President of National Constituent Assembly of short-lived revival of Union of Central American Republics.
	Bustamante appointed member of International Court of Justice in Hague.
	Panama: dispute with Costa Rica provokes US intervention.
	Bustamante proposes Pan-American League to resolve disputes between countries.
	Haiti: Guilbaud recalled to his country.
1922	Panama: Burgos appointed Minister to Italy and Switzerland.
	Honduras: Carías Presidency begins (to 1948).
	Haiti: General John H Russell becomes High Commissioner; runs Haiti in tandem with President Louis Borno.
	US Secretary of State Charles Hughes hosts Central American Nationals Conference to establish cooperation between states and tribunal for settling disputes.

YEAR	HISTORY	CULTURE
1920	League of Nations comes into existence.	F Scott Fitzgerald, *This Side of Paradise.*
	The Hague selected as seat of International Court of Justice.	Franz Kafka, *The Country Doctor.*
	Bolsheviks win Russian Civil War.	Rambert School of Ballet formed.
	Adolf Hitler announces 25-point programme in Munich.	Lyonel Feininger, *Church.*
		Maurice Ravel, *La Valse.*
1921	Irish Free State established.	Aldous Huxley, *Crome Yellow.*
	Peace treaty signed between Russia and Germany.	D H Lawrence, *Women in Love.*
	State of Emergency proclaimed in Germany in face of economic crisis.	Sergei Prokofiev, *The Love for Three Oranges.*
	Washington Naval Treaty signed.	
1922	Chanak crisis.	T S Eliot, *The Waste Land.*
	Britain recognises Kingdom of Egypt under Fuad I.	James Joyce, *Ulysses.*
	Gandhi sentenced to six years in prison for civil disobedience.	F Scott Fitzgerald, *The Beautiful and Damned.*
		Hermann Hesse, *Siddhartha.*
	Election in Irish Free State gives majority to Pro-Treaty candidates.	Clive Bell, *Since Cezanne.*
		Irving Berlin, *April Showers.*
	League of Nations Council approves British Mandate in Palestine.	British Broadcasting Company (later Corporation) (BBC) founded.

YEAR	THE LIVES AND THE LANDS
1923	Honduras: Policarpo Bonilla fails in attempt to be elected President; Lopez Gutiérrez declares himself President; civil war breaks out.
	Conference of American States at Santiago discusses Pan-American League (no resolution), agrees mechanism for resolving Pan-American disputes.
	Haiti: Guilbaud retires from public office.
1924	Guatemala: Cabrera's overthrow leads to regime of Generals Orellana and Chacón.
	Cuba: Gerardo Machado y Morales elected President, begins rule of repression.
1925	Bustamante publishes *The World Court.*
	Nicaragua: US Marines temporary withdrawal; uprising follows, settled by US intervention in 1927 and establishment of National Guard.
1926	11 September: Policarpo Bonilla dies in New Orleans aged 68.

YEAR	HISTORY	CULTURE
1923	French and Belgian troops occupy the Ruhr when Germany fails to make reparation payments. The USSR formally comes into existence. State of Emergency declared in Germany. British Mandate in Palestine begins. Adolf Hitler's *coup d'état* (The Beer Hall Putsch) fails.	François Mauriac, *Genitrix.* P G Wodehouse, *The Inimitable Jeeves.* Sigmund Freud, *The Ego and the Id.* Max Beckmann, *The Trapeze.* Mark Chagall, *Love Idyll.* George Gershwin, *Rhapsody in Blue.* Bela Bartok, *Dance Suite.*
1924	Dawes Plan published. Turkish National Assembly expels Ottoman dynasty. Greece proclaimed republic. Nazi party enters German Reichstag.	E M Forster, *A Passage to India.* George Bernard Shaw, *St Joan.* 'The Blue Four' expressionist group is formed.
1925	Paul von Hindenburg, former military leader, elected President of Germany.	Franz Kafka, *The Trial.* Virginia Woolf, *Mrs Dalloway.* Film: *Battleship Potemkin.*
1926	General Strike in Britain. France proclaims the Lebanon a republic. Germany is admitted into League of Nations; Spain leaves as result. Leon Trotsky and Grigory Zinoviev expelled from Politburo of Communist Party following Josef Stalin's victory in USSR.	Franz Kafka, *The Castle.* A A Milne, *Winnie the Pooh.* Ernest Hemingway, *The Sun Also Rises.* Sean O'Casey, *The Plough and The Stars.* Edvard Munch, *The Red House.* Giacomo Puccini, *Turandot.*

YEAR	THE LIVES AND THE LANDS
1928	Bustamante is President of Sixth International Conference of American States in Havana; Conference agrees to adopt his work on international private law – becomes known as Bustamante Code.
1929	Haiti: Forbes Commission of Inquiry after US Marines kill civilians at Hayes recommends phased withdrawal by US.
1930	Bustamante re-elected member of International Court of Justice in the Hague.
1931	Guatemala: Jorge Ubico becomes President; begins 13 years of autocratic rule.

YEAR	HISTORY	CULTURE
1928	Transjordan becomes self-governing under British Mandate.	D H Lawrence, *Lady Chatterley's Lover*.
	Kellogg-Briand Pact outlawing war and providing for peaceful settlement of disputes signed.	Aldous Huxley, *Point Counterpoint*.
	Albania proclaimed Kingdom.	Max Beckmann, *Black Lillies*.
	Alexander Fleming discovers penicillin.	Henri Matisse, *Seated Odalisque*.
		George Gershwin, *An American in Paris*.
		Kurt Weill, *The Threepenny Opera*.
1929	Fascists win single-party elections in Italy.	Jean Cocteau, *Les Enfants Terribles*.
	Germany accepts Young Plan at Reparations Conference in the Hague – Allies agree to evacuate the Rhineland.	Ernest Hemingway, *A Farewell to Arms*.
		Erich Maria Remarque, *All Quiet on the Western Front*.
	Wall Street Crash	Marc Chagall, *Love Idyll*.
1930	Britain, France, Italy, Japan and US sign London Naval Treaty regulating naval expansion.	T S Eliot, *Ash Wednesday*.
		W H Auden, *Poems*.
	Acrylic plastics invented.	Noel Coward, *Private Lives*.
		Igor Stravinsky, *Symphony of Psalms*.
1931	Delhi Pact between Viceroy of India and Gandhi suspends civil disobedience campaign.	Noel Coward, *Cavalcade*.
		William Faulkner, *Sanctuary*.
	Bankruptcy of Credit-Anstalt in Austria begins Central Europe's financial collapse.	Robert Frost, *Collected Poems*.
		Salvador Dali, *The Persistence of Memory*.

YEAR	THE LIVES AND THE LANDS
1933	Nicaragua: US troops finally leave.

1934 Panama: Burgos appointed Minister to Cuba.

Haiti: 15 August, United States troops finally pull out.

Nicaragua. Augusto César Sandino murdered by National Guard; its chief Anastasio Somoza becomes dominant figure in country for next 22 years.

Cuba: Fulgencio Batista emerges as new strongman in Cuba; new trade agreement signed with US.

1937 2 August: Burgos dies of cerebral haemorrhage in Rome aged 64.

Haiti: thousands of Haitian civilians massacred by Dominican Republic troops.

1939 19 September: Guilbaud dies in Port-au-Prince aged 83.

YEAR	HISTORY	CULTURE
1933	Adolf Hitler appointed Chancellor of Germany.	George Orwell, *Down and Out in Paris and London.*
	Germany withdraws from League of Nations, Disarmament Conference.	Films: *Duck Soup. King Kong. Queen Christina.*
1934	Anglo-Russian Trade Agreement.	F Scott Fitzgerald, *Tender Is the Night.*
	General strike staged in France.	Robert Graves, *I, Claudius.*
	Germany, 'Night of the Long Knives'.	Dmitri Shostakovich, *Lady Macbeth of Mtsensk.*
	After German President Hindenburg dies, role of President and Chancellor merged; Hitler becomes *Führer.*	Sergei Rakhmaninov, *Rhapsody on a Theme of Paganini.*
		Jean Cocteau, *La Machine Infernale.*
	USSR admitted to League of Nations.	Salvador Dali, *William Tell.*
	Kirov is assassinated in USSR.	John Dewey, *Art as Experience.*
	Japan repudiates Washington Treaties of 1922 and 1930.	Films: *David Copperfield.*
1937	UK Royal Commission on Palestine recommends partition into British and Arab areas and Jewish state.	Jean-Paul Sartre, *Nausea.*
		John Steinbeck, *Of Mice and Men.*
	Italy joins German-Japanese Anti-Comintern Pact.	Films: *Snow White and the Seven Dwarfs. A Star is Born.*
1939	Italy invades Albania.	Bela Bartok, *String Quartet No. 6.*
	Hitler and Mussolini sign Pact of Steel.	James Joyce, *Finnegan's Wake.*
	Nazi-Soviet Pact agrees no fighting, partition of Poland.	John Steinbeck, *The Grapes of Wrath.*
	Second World War begins (ends in 1945): Germany invades Poland: Britain and France declare war.	Films: *Gone with the Wind. The Wizard of Oz.*

YEAR	THE LIVES AND THE LANDS
1941	Panama: Arnulfo Arias deposed as President in coup. Honduras: declares war on Japan and Germany. Cuba, Guatemala, Haiti and Panama: declare war on Germany, Japan and Italy. Nicaragua: follows US declaring war on Japan and Germany; allows US bases on Nicaraguan soil.
1942	Haiti: allows US to site patrol base to help safeguard Windward Passage; after war signs Military Assistance Agreement with US. Cuba: grants US facilities to carry out operation against German submarines.
1943	28 September: Méndez dies in Guatemala City aged 82.
1944	Guatemala: Ubico forced to quit power after popular revolt; free elections and reforms, including land redistribution, follow.

YEAR	HISTORY	CULTURE
1941	Germany invades USSR. Japan attacks Pearl Harbor. Germany and Italy declare war on US.	Bertold Brecht, *Mother Courage and Her Children*. Noel Coward, *Blithe Spirit*.
1942	Singapore surrenders to Japanese. US surrender in Philippines. US Guadalcanal invasion turns Japanese tide. Battle of Stalingrad.	Dmitri Shostakovich, *Symphony No. 7*. Albert Camus, *The Outsider*. T S Eliot, *Little Gidding*.
1943	Romanians and Germans surrender to Russians at Stalingrad. Allies demand unconditional surrender from Germany and Japan at Casablanca Conference. Italy surrenders unconditionally. Tehran Conference.	Albert Hoffman discovers LSD. Jean-Paul Sartre, *Being and Nothingness*. Henry Moore, *Madonna and Child*. Richard Rogers and Oscar Hammerstein, *Oklahoma!* Jean-Paul Sartre, *The Flies*.
1944	D-Day landings in France. Claus von Stauffenberg's bomb at Rastenburg fails to kill Hitler. Free French enter Paris. German counter-offensive in the Ardennes.	Carl Jung, *Psychology and Religion*. Michael Tippett, *A Child of Our Time*. T S Eliot, *Four Quartets*. Terrence Rattigan, *The Winslow Boy*. Tennessee Williams, *The Glass Menagerie*.

YEAR	THE LIVES AND THE LANDS
1951	24 August Bustamante dies in Havana aged 86.
1954	Guatemala: government of Jacobo Arbenz overthrown with help of US; Armas installed as President in counter-revolutionary government.
1955	Panama: New agreement with US over Canal Zone (sovereignty agreed in 1977, passing to Panama in 1999).

YEAR	HISTORY	CULTURE
1951	Korean War.	Henry Moore, *Reclining Figure.*
	Peace Treaty with Japan signed by 49 powers, though not USSR.	Benjamin Britten, *Billy Budd.*
		Igor Stravinsky, *The Rake's Progress.*
	Libya becomes independent federation.	J D Salinger, *The Catcher in the Rye.*
	Electric power is produced from atomic energy in USA.	Herman Wouk, *The Caine Mutiny.*
1954	Tito elected first President of Yugoslav Republic.	Benjamin Britten, *The Turn of the Screw.*
	European Political Community Constitution drafted, later adopted.	Kingsley Amis, *Lucky Jim.*
		William Golding, *Lord of the Flies.*
		J R R Tolkein, *The Lord of the Rings I, II.* (*III* in 1955)
		Tennessee Williams, *Cat on a Hot Tin Roof.*
1955	USSR declares end of war with Germany.	Vladimir Nabokov, *Lolita.*
	Winston Churchill resigns as British Prime Minister; replaced by Anthony Eden.	Samuel Beckett, *Waiting for Godot.*
		Films: *The Seven Year Itch. Rebel Without A Cause. The Ladykillers.*
	Armistice for Indochina signed: France evacuates North Vietnam; Ho Chi Minh forms government.	Sony launches first mass-produced transistor radio.
		Commercial television introduced in Britain.

YEAR	THE LIVES AND THE LANDS

1956   Nicaragua: Anastasio Somoza assassinated; succeeded by sons (who rule to 1979).

Cuba: Fidel and Raul Castro, and Che Guevara land; begin assault to take power.

1957   Haiti: François 'Papa Doc' Duvalier becomes President; instigates brutal autocratic regime, ruling until his death in 1971.

Honduras: dictator Lozana Diaz deposed; Liberal Morales wins election; rules to 1963 when period of military rule instigated.

1959   Cuba: Fidel Castro takes power after long guerrilla war.

YEAR	HISTORY	CULTURE
1956	Pakistan becomes independent. USSR abolishes Cominform. UN obtains agreements of ceasefire between Israel and Jordan; Lebanon; Syria. Suez Crisis. Hungary renounces Warsaw Treaty; Soviet forces attack Budapest.	Karl Mannheim, *Essays on the Sociology of Culture.* First computer-programming language invented in USA. A J Ayer, *The Problem of Knowledge.* Benjamin Britten, *The Prince of the Pagodas.* Alan J Lerner & Frederick Lowe, *My Fair Lady.* John Osborne, *Look Back in Anger.*
1957	Belgium, France, West Germany, Italy, Luxembourg, the Netherlands sign Treaty of Rome establishing the European Economic Community (EEC). US, Britain, France, West Germany issue declaration on principles of German reunification, call for free elections.	Kenneth Clark, *The Nude.* Jack Kerouac, *On the Road.* Patrick White, *Voss.* Samuel Beckett, *Endgame.* Leonard Bernstein, *West Side Story.* Francis Poulenc, *Les Dialogues des Carmelites.* Francis Bacon, *Screaming Nurse.*
1959	UN votes against admission of People's Republic of China. UN General Assembly condemns Apartheid in South Africa and all other racial discrimination. Stockholm Conference: Finance Ministers of Austria, Denmark, Britain, Norway, Portugal, Sweden, Switzerland establish European Free Trade Association.	Günther Grass, *The Tin Drum.* Brendan Behan, *The Hostage.* Harold Pinter, *The Caretaker.* Richard Rodgers & Oscar Hammerstein, *The Sound of Music.* Motown Records founded in Detroit, USA.

Further Reading

Cuba, Guatemala, Haiti, Honduras, Nicaragua and Panama
There is no shortage of general histories about Central America, though many are to be found as sections of histories of Latin America as a whole. For a very brief outline from pre-colonial times to the middle of the 20th century, George Pendle's A *History of Latin America* (Penguin, 1969) is still a valuable read for beginners as it includes sections on Central America and the Caribbean. The best detailed survey of the colonial history of the region and then independence up to the second half of the 18th century remains the *Cambridge History of Latin America* Volumes I –III (Cambridge, 1985), edited by Leslie Bethell. For a detailed and authoritative account of the wars of independence see *The Spanish American Revolutions 1808–1826* (Norton, 1986) by John Lynch. *Latin America, Economy and Society 1870–1930* (Cambridge, 1989), edited by Leslie Bethell, provides a fascinating insight into the period, though it is not light reading. A more accessible and more general history can be found in *Modern Latin America* by Thomas E. Skidmore and Peter H. Smith (OUP, 1989). Among works specifically on Central America, the most accessible is Ralph Lee Woodward Jr's excellent

Central America: A Nation Divided (Oxford, 1985), which ranges from pre-Conquest times to the late 20th century.

Cambridge University Press's *Latin America since 1930: Mexico, Central America and the Caribbean*, edited by Leslie Bethell, is also essential reading. For a different take on Central America that moves away from the usual emphasis on the United States, Thomas D Schoonover's *The French in Central America: Culture and Commerce 1820–1930* (Scholarly Resources, 2000) is recommended.

Selden Rodman's *The Guatemala Traveller: A Concise History and Guide* (New York, 1971) is a useful introduction to that country, as is James A Morris' *Honduras: Caudillo Politics and Military Rulers* (Westview Press, 1984). H K Meyer's *Historical Dictionary of Nicaragua* (Scarecrow Press, 1972) covers the basics of Nicaraguan history, while *The Panama Story* (Metropolitan Press, 1968) by John Niemeier does the same for Panamanian history.

For Cuba, Marifeli Pérez-Stable's *The Cuban Revolution: Origins, Course and Legacy* (Oxford, 1993) is an important book, while *Haiti and the Great Powers 1902–1915* (Louisiana State University, 1988) by Brenda Gayle Plummer covers a tumultuous period in that country's history, as does Hans Schmidt's *The United States Occupation of Haiti 1915–1934* (Rutgers University Press, 1971).

Foreign relations

For a general work covering North, South and Central America, J Lloyd Mecham's *A Survey of United States-Latin American Relations* (Houghton Mifflin, 1965) is an insightful read, though it sees the relationship very much from an American point of view. In contrast, *Under the Eagle: U.S. Intervention in Central America and the Caribbean* (South

End Press, 1981) by Jenny Pearce gives a very lively and critical account of American activity in the region. More measured is George Black's *The Good Neighbor: How the United States Wrote the History of Central America and the Caribbean* (Pantheon, 1988). *The Banana Wars: United States Intervention in the Caribbean 1898–1934* (Dorsey Press, 1983) by Lester D Langley focuses on the fruit barons, while *U.S. Foreign Policy in the Caribbean, Cuba and Central America* (Praeger, 1985) by James N and James W Cortada focuses more on policy issues. Essential reading is Dana G Monro's *Intervention and Dollar Diplomacy in the Caribbean 1900–1921* (Princeton, 1964), which is enhanced by the author's own diplomatic experience of the region at the time.

Central America, the Paris Peace Conference and the Treaty of Versailles

It has to be stated from the outset that outside national government archives, specific material on Central American and Caribbean countries, the Paris Peace Conference and the Treaty of Versailles is hard to come by. However, in addition to the above titles there are some works that deal with the war and events immediately afterwards. The most useful is still Percy Martin's *Latin America and the War* (Johns Hopkins, 1925) which, despite its age and the fact that it is sometimes a little uncritical, is still a marvellous survey of how the countries of Central and South America responded to the war. As its title suggests, *The Aftermath of War: World War I and US Policy Toward Latin America* (New York University Press, 1971) by Joseph L Tulchin covers the end of the war and the years immediately afterwards.

An excellent and concise introduction to the Conference is Alan Sharp's *The Versailles Settlement: Peacemaking in Paris,*

1919 (Macmillan,1991; second edition 2008). A lengthier account is Margaret MacMillan's compelling *Paris 1919: Six Months That Changed the World* (Random House, 2001), which manages to capture the mood of the city at the time of the Conference as well as the negotiations themselves. Lord Riddell's *Intimate Diary of the Peace Conference and After 1918–1923* (Victor Gollancz, 1933) is an account by someone who was on the fringes of the Conference, but who was in regular contact with the British delegation, including David Lloyd George. An insider's view from an American perspective can be found in *What Really Happened at Paris: The Story of the Peace Conference 1918–1919* (Charles Scribner's,1921) by Edward Mandell House and Charles Seymour. Excerpts of writings from historians and politicians concerning the Conference and the subsequent Treaty are contained in *The Treaty of Versailles* (Greenhaven, 2001) edited by Jeff Hay. Analysis of the peace process from an American viewpoint is found in *Woodrow Wilson and the Paris Peace Conference* (D C Heath, 1972) edited by N Gordon Levin, Jr. Thomas A Bailey's *Woodrow Wilson and The Lost Peace* (Macmillan, 1944) examines the role of Wilson and also American public opinion. *A Time for Angels* (Alfred A Knopf, 1975) by Elmer Bendiner is a lively account of the creation and ultimately the demise of the League of Nations.

Picture Sources

The author and publishers wish to express their thanks to the following sources of illustrative material and/or permission to reproduce it. They will make proper acknowledgements in future editions in the event that any omissions have occurred.

Corbis and Topham Picturepoint.

Endpapers
The Signing of Peace in the Hall of Mirrors, Versailles, 28th June 1919 by Sir William Orpen (Imperial War Museum: akg-images)
Front row: Dr Johannes Bell (Germany) signing with Herr Hermann Müller leaning over him
Middle row (seated, left to right): General Tasker H Bliss, Col E M House, Mr Henry White, Mr Robert Lansing, President Woodrow Wilson (United States); M Georges Clemenceau (France); Mr David Lloyd George, Mr Andrew Bonar Law, Mr Arthur J Balfour, Viscount Milner, Mr G N Barnes (Great Britain); Prince Saionji (Japan)
Back row (left to right): M Eleftherios Venizelos (Greece);

Dr Afonso Costa (Portugal); Lord Riddell (British Press); Sir George E Foster (Canada); M Nikola Pašić (Serbia); M Stephen Pichon (France); Col Sir Maurice Hankey, Mr Edwin S Montagu (Great Britain); the Maharajah of Bikaner (India); Signor Vittorio Emanuele Orlando (Italy); M Paul Hymans (Belgium); General Louis Botha (South Africa); Mr W M Hughes (Australia)

Jacket images

(Front): Imperial War Museum: akg Images.
(Back): *Peace Conference at the Quai d'Orsay* by Sir William Orpen (Imperial War Museum: akg Images).
Left to right (seated): Signor Orlando (Italy); Mr Robert Lansing, President Woodrow Wilson (United States); M Georges Clemenceau (France); Mr David Lloyd George, Mr Andrew Bonar Law, Mr Arthur J Balfour (Great Britain); Left to right (standing): M Paul Hymans (Belgium); Mr Eleftherios Venizelos (Greece); The Emir Feisal (The Hashemite Kingdom); Mr W F Massey (New Zealand); General Jan Smuts (South Africa); Col E M House (United States); General Louis Botha (South Africa); Prince Saionji (Japan); Mr W M Hughes (Australia); Sir Robert Borden (Canada); Mr G N Barnes (Great Britain); M Ignacy Paderewski (Poland)

Index

Makers
of the
Modern
World

UK PUBLICATION: November 2008 to December 2010
CLASSIFICATION: Biography/History/
    International Relations
FORMAT: 198 × 128mm
EXTENT: 208pp
ILLUSTRATIONS: 6 photographs plus 4 maps
TERRITORY: world

Chronology of life in context, full index, bibliography innovative layout
with sidebars

Woodrow Wilson: United States of America by Brian Morton
Friedrich Ebert: Germany by Harry Harmer
Georges Clemenceau: France by David Watson
David Lloyd George: Great Britain by Alan Sharp
Prince Saionji: Japan by Jonathan Clements
Wellington Koo: China by Jonathan Clements
Eleftherios Venizelos: Greece by Andrew Dalby
From the Sultan to Atatürk: Turkey by Andrew Mango
The Hashemites: The Dream of Arabia by Robert McNamara
Chaim Weizmann: The Dream of Zion by Tom Fraser
Piip, Meierovics & Voldemaras: Estonia, Latvia & Lithuania by Charlotte Alston
Ignacy Paderewski: Poland by Anita Prazmowska
Beneš, Masaryk: Czechoslovakia by Peter Neville
Károlyi & Bethlen: Hungary by Bryan Cartledge
Karl Renner: Austria by Jamie Bulloch
Vittorio Orlando: Italy by Spencer Di Scala
Pašić & Trumbić: The Kingdom of Serbs, Croats and Slovenes by Dejan Djokic
Aleksandŭr Stamboliĭski: Bulgaria by R J Crampton
Ion Bratianu: Romania by Keith Hitchin
Paul Hymans: Belgium by Sally Marks
General Smuts: South Africa by Antony Lentin
William Hughes: Australia by Carl Bridge
William Massey: New Zealand by James Watson
Sir Robert Borden: Canada by Martin Thornton
Maharajah of Bikaner: India by Hugh Purcell
Afonso Costa: Portugal by Filipe Ribeiro de Meneses
Epitácio Pessoa: Brazil by Michael Streeter
South America by Michael Streeter
Central America by Michael Streeter
South East Asia by Andrew Dalby
The League of Nations by Ruth Henig
Consequences of Peace: The Versailles Settlement – Aftermath and Legacy
    by Alan Sharp